First World War
and Army of Occupation
War Diary
France, Belgium and Germany

52 DIVISION
157 Infantry Brigade
Highland Light Infantry
7th (Blythswood) Battalion (Territorial)
1 April 1918 - 30 April 1919

WO95/2898/4

The Naval & Military Press Ltd
www.nmarchive.com
Published in association with The National Archives

Published by

The Naval & Military Press Ltd

Unit 10 Ridgewood Industrial Park,

Uckfield, East Sussex,

TN22 5QE England

Tel: +44 (0) 1825 749494

www.naval-military-press.com

www.nmarchive.com

This diary has been reprinted in facsimile from the original. Any imperfections are inevitably reproduced and the quality may fall short of modern type and cartographic standards.

© Crown Copyright
Images reproduced by permission of The National Archives, London, England, 2015.

Contents

Document type	Place/Title	Date From	Date To
Heading	WO95/2898-4		
Heading	52nd Division 157th Infy Bde 1-7th Br. Highland Lt Infy Apr 1918-Apr 1919		
Heading	157th Brigade 52nd Division Disembarked Marseilles From Egypt 17.4.18. 1/7th Battalion Highland Light Infantry April 1918.		
Heading	War Diary For April 1918 Volume III		
War Diary	C 28 a-O	01/04/1918	02/04/1918
War Diary	Sarona	03/04/1918	03/04/1918
War Diary	Surafend	04/04/1918	06/04/1918
War Diary	Kantara	07/04/1918	07/04/1918
War Diary	Sidi Bish	08/04/1918	09/04/1918
War Diary	Alexandria	10/04/1918	10/04/1918
War Diary	At Sea	11/04/1918	16/04/1918
War Diary	Montfuront	17/04/1918	19/04/1918
War Diary	Tn Train	20/04/1918	21/04/1918
War Diary	Noyelles	22/04/1918	23/04/1918
War Diary	Cayeux	24/04/1918	28/04/1918
War Diary	La Lacque	29/04/1918	30/04/1918
Miscellaneous	Summary Of Casualties During April 1918		
Miscellaneous	1/7th (Blythswood) Battalion The Highland Light Infantry Move Orders No. 7	31/08/1918	31/08/1918
Operation(al) Order(s)	1/7th (Blythswood) Battalion The Highland Light Infantry Battalion Order No. 288	02/04/1918	02/04/1918
Miscellaneous	1/7th (Blythswood) Battalion The Highland Light Infantry Battalion Orders	28/04/1918	28/04/1918
Heading	War Diary 1/7th H.L.I 1st-31st May 1918 Volume III		
War Diary	La Lacque	01/05/1918	06/05/1918
War Diary	Maroeuil	07/05/1918	07/05/1918
War Diary	Vimy	08/05/1918	24/05/1918
War Diary	St Eloy	25/05/1918	31/05/1918
Miscellaneous	Summary Of Casualties For May 1918		
Miscellaneous	1/7th (Blythswood) Battalion The Highland Light Infantry Battalion Orders	05/05/1918	05/05/1918
Miscellaneous	Copy No.9	14/05/1918	14/05/1918
Miscellaneous	1/7th (Blythswood) Battalion The Highland Light Infantry Battalion Orders	14/05/1918	14/05/1918
Miscellaneous	1/7th (Blythswood) Battalion The Highland Light Infantry Battalion Orders	19/05/1918	19/05/1918
Miscellaneous	1/7th (Blythswood) Battalion The Highland Light Infantry Battalion Orders	23/05/1918	23/05/1918
Heading	1/7th H.L.I War Diary June 1918 Vol 3		
War Diary	St. Eloy	01/06/1918	02/06/1918
War Diary	Willerval Section	03/06/1918	20/06/1918
War Diary	St. Eloy	21/06/1918	28/06/1918
War Diary	Vimy	29/06/1918	30/06/1918
Miscellaneous	Summary Of Casualties For June 1918		
Miscellaneous	1/7th (Blythswood) Battalion The Highland Light Infantry Battalion Orders	01/06/1918	01/06/1918
Miscellaneous	Warning Orders	27/06/1918	27/06/1918

Type	Description	Date From	Date To
Miscellaneous	1/7th (Blythswood) Battalion The Highland Light Infantry Battalion Orders	07/06/1918	07/06/1918
Miscellaneous	1/7th (Blythswood) Battalion The Highland Light Infantry Battalion Orders	13/06/1918	13/06/1918
Miscellaneous	1/7th (Blythswood) Battalion The Highland Light Infantry Battalion Orders	19/06/1918	19/06/1918
Miscellaneous	Administrative Instructions	19/06/1918	19/06/1918
Heading	War Diary Volume III July 1st To 31st 1918		
War Diary	Vimy	01/07/1918	16/07/1918
War Diary	St. Eloy	17/07/1918	19/07/1918
War Diary	Auchel	20/07/1918	31/07/1918
Miscellaneous	1/7th (Blythswood) Battalion-The Highland Light Infantry Battalion Orders	10/07/1918	10/07/1918
Miscellaneous	1/7th (Blythswood) Battalion-The Highland Light Infantry Battalion Orders	14/07/1918	14/07/1918
Miscellaneous	1/7th (Blythswood) Battalion-The Highland Light Infantry Battalion Orders	15/07/1918	15/07/1918
Miscellaneous	Administrative Instructions Issued With Battalion Orders	15/07/1918	15/07/1918
Miscellaneous	1/7th (Blythswood) Battalion The Highland Light Infantry Warning Order		
Miscellaneous	After Order By Major E Watson M.C. Commanding	15/07/1918	15/07/1918
Miscellaneous	1/7th Bn. Highland Light Infantry Move Orders	19/07/1918	19/07/1918
Heading	War Diary Volume III August 1st To 31st 1918		
War Diary	Oppy Section	01/08/1918	16/08/1918
War Diary	Mont St Eloy	17/08/1918	17/08/1918
War Diary	Marqueffles Camp	18/08/1918	20/08/1918
War Diary	Aignez Les Duisans	21/08/1918	22/08/1918
War Diary	Bellacourt	23/08/1918	23/08/1918
War Diary	Ficheux	24/08/1918	24/08/1918
War Diary	Near Henin	25/08/1918	31/08/1918
Miscellaneous	1/7th Bn. Highland Light Infantry Move Orders	01/08/1918	01/08/1918
Miscellaneous	Copy No.6	07/08/1918	07/08/1918
Miscellaneous	1/7th (Blythswood) Battalion-The Highland Light Infantry Battalion Orders	05/08/1918	05/08/1918
Miscellaneous	1/7th (Blythswood) Battalion-The Highland Light Infantry Battalion Orders	06/08/1918	06/08/1918
Miscellaneous	1/7th Bn. The Highland Light Infantry Move Orders	19/08/1918	19/08/1918
Miscellaneous	1/7th (Blythswood) Battalion-The Highland Light Infantry Move Orders No.3	16/08/1918	16/08/1918
Heading	1/7th H.L.I Vol.6 War Diary For September 1918		
War Diary	Near Mercatel	01/09/1918	01/09/1918
War Diary	Henin Hill	02/09/1918	02/09/1918
War Diary	Hindenburg Line (N. of Bullecourt)	03/09/1918	03/09/1918
War Diary	Near Pronville	04/09/1918	06/09/1918
War Diary	NE Croisilles	07/09/1918	16/09/1918
War Diary	Inchy-En-Artois	17/09/1918	19/09/1918
War Diary	Near Noreuil	20/09/1918	25/09/1918
War Diary	Near Queant	26/09/1918	26/09/1918
War Diary	Near E Moeuvres	27/09/1918	30/09/1918
War Diary	Summary Of Casualties For September 1918		
Operation(al) Order(s)	1/7th H.L.I Battalion Orders No.1	19/09/1918	19/09/1918
Miscellaneous	1/7th Bn. H.L.I. Move Orders No.7	16/09/1918	16/09/1918
Miscellaneous	1/7th Bn. (Blythswood) Battalion The Highland Light Infantry Orders	19/09/1918	19/09/1918
Miscellaneous	1/7th (Blythswood) Bn. Highland Light Infantry Battalion Orders	25/09/1918	25/09/1918

Type	Description	Date From	Date To
Miscellaneous	1/7th (Blythswood) Battalion-The Highland Light Infantry Move Orders No.3	30/09/1918	30/09/1918
Heading	7th Batt. H.L.I. War Diary For Month Of October 1918		
War Diary	Near Mouvres	01/10/1918	01/10/1918
War Diary	Near Canal De L'Esceaut F 30c	02/10/1918	04/10/1918
War Diary	Near Canal De L'Esceaut F30 A	05/10/1918	05/10/1918
War Diary	Near Moeuvres	06/10/1918	07/10/1918
War Diary	Petit Houvin & Liencourt	08/10/1918	08/10/1918
War Diary	Liencourt	09/10/1918	19/10/1918
War Diary	Mount St. Eloy	20/10/1918	20/10/1918
War Diary	Henin Lietard	21/10/1918	21/10/1918
War Diary	Flers	22/10/1918	24/10/1918
War Diary	Flines	25/10/1918	30/10/1918
War Diary	Rue Bouchin J.19	31/10/1918	31/10/1918
Miscellaneous	1/7th (Blythswood) Battalion-The Highland Light Infantry Move Orders No.3	30/09/1918	30/09/1918
Operation(al) Order(s)	1/7th (Blythswood) Battalion-The Highland Light Infantry Order No. 5	07/10/1918	07/10/1918
Operation(al) Order(s)	1/7th (Blythswood) Battalion The Highland Light Infantry Move Orders No.6	19/10/1918	19/10/1918
Operation(al) Order(s)	1/7th (Blythswood) Battalion-The Highland Light Infantry Move Order No. 7	19/10/1918	19/10/1918
Operation(al) Order(s)	Battalion Orders No.8 By Lieut Col J.H. Foster Commanding	23/10/1918	23/10/1918
Operation(al) Order(s)	Battalion Orders. No.9 By Lieut Col J.H. Foster Commanding	23/10/1918	23/10/1918
Operation(al) Order(s)	Battalion Orders No.10 By Lieut Col J.H. Foster Commanding	26/10/1918	26/10/1918
Operation(al) Order(s)	Battalion Orders No.11 By Lieut Col J.H. Foster Commanding	27/10/1918	27/10/1918
Heading	7th Batt. H.L.I. War Diary For November 1918		
War Diary	La Bouchin J 19	01/11/1918	04/11/1918
War Diary	Near Fresnes	05/11/1918	08/11/1918
War Diary	Vieux Conde	09/11/1918	09/11/1918
War Diary	Pommeroeuil	10/11/1918	10/11/1918
War Diary	Near Ghlin	11/11/1918	11/11/1918
War Diary	Vacresse	12/11/1918	15/11/1918
War Diary	Maisieres	16/11/1918	30/11/1918
Operation(al) Order(s)	1/7th (Blythewood) Battalion The Highland Light Infantry Order No. 19	04/11/1918	04/11/1918
Operation(al) Order(s)	1/7th (Blythswood) Battalion The Highland Light Infantry Order No. 13	07/11/1918	07/11/1918
Operation(al) Order(s)	1/7th (Blythswood) Battalion The Highland Light Infantry Order No. 14	07/11/1918	07/11/1918
Operation(al) Order(s)	1/7th (Blythswood) Battalion The Highland Light Infantry Battalion Order No. 17	14/11/1918	14/11/1918
War Diary	Maisieres	01/12/1918	21/03/1919
War Diary	Soignies	22/03/1919	31/03/1919
Miscellaneous	Summary Of Casualties For March 1919		
Miscellaneous	War Office	15/05/1919	15/05/1919
War Diary	Soignies	01/04/1919	28/04/1919
War Diary	Dunkirk	30/04/1919	30/04/1919

3095/2898(4)

3047/2898(4)

52ND DIVISION
157TH INFY BDE

1-7TH BN HIGHLAND LT INFY.
APR 1918-APR 1919

157th Brigade.

52nd Division.

Disembarked MARSEILLES from EGYPT 17.4.18.

1/7th BATTALION

HIGHLAND LIGHT INFANTRY

APRIL 1918.

2. I
6 sheets

1/7. H.L.I. 1896

War Diary

for April 1918.

Volume III.

Army Form C. 2118.

WAR DIARY
or
INTELLIGENCE SUMMARY.

(Erase heading not required.)

Volume VII
1st to 30th April 1918.

1/7th H.L.I.

Ref Map ARSUF K6

Place	Date	Hour	Summary of Events and Information	Remarks and references to Appendices
C.28a-0	1/4/18		Ration Strength 32 Officers 668 O.Rs. (1 Officer 185 ORs returned unfit) Effective Strength 43 Officers & 945 ORs.	
do	2/4/18		A quiet day only a little shelling by Ert Sector. No Cas. 2/Lt AWB Quiet day. 5/Lt 10th W.R. & 2 ORs Black Watch & 5 JRD Return home interred by the 6th Bn. RS. Black Watch at 2200 when relieved we marched to	
SARONA	3/4/18		SARONA arriving about 0200 AWB Left at 1830 and marched to SURAFEND	
SURAFEND	4/4/18		Return of Entrenching Stores 28 ORs from Pioneer Orchard & Lt R.E.A. MILLER from Lewis Gun Course	Relief about 2245. From hospital 5 ORs # AWB
do	5/4/18		SURAFEND morning about 2245. From hospital 5 ORs # AWB	To ex.p. 1 Off.
do	6/6/18		Return of Animals AWB	AWB
KANTARA	7/4/18		Entrained at LUDD at 0920 for KANTARA AWB Arrived at 0844 and marched to No.1 I.B.D. Entrained at 2200 for ALEXANDRA 2/Lt W. MACKIE and 87 ORs from hosp. 8 ORs detach. after regiments exchanged	
SIDI BISH STAFF	8/4/18		Rejoined 2/Lt RIDDEHOUGH R.A.M.C. also had joined on & met former 15 Lg Cas	
do	9/4/18		Arrived at 0720 O/C & R.F.C. & Commander Col. R. & J. Boyd from home leave AWB Embarked 28 Officers and 937 ORs at Alexandria & board HMT INDARRA AWB	
ALEXANDRIA	10/4/18		Lay in harbour AWB	
At Sea	11/4/18		Sailed at 1430 AWB	
At Sea	12/4/18 to 15/4/18		At Sea AWB	
MONTFERRAT	16/4/18		Arrived at MARSEILLES at 6.30 and went into camp. 30 O.Rs. 13 ORs AWB	

2353 Wt. W2544/1454 700,000 5/15 D. D. & L.   A.D.S.S./Forms/C. 2118.

Army Form C. 2118.

WAR DIARY
or
INTELLIGENCE SUMMARY.
(Erase heading not required.)

Volume III

17th A.T.T.

1st to 30th April 1918

Place	Date	Hour	Summary of Events and Information	Remarks and references to Appendices
MONTFLEURET	18/4/18		Remained in Camp. AM3	
do	19/4/18		do — do — 3 O.R.S. AM3	
In TRAIN	20/4/18		To bed 3 O.R. AM3	
	21/4/18		In train AM3	
NOYELLES	22/4/18		Arrived at NOYELLES and marched to Camp. AM3	
do	23/4/18		Paraded at 07.30 and marched to CAYEUX arrg at 12.30. AM3	
CAYEUX	24/4/18		Gas training. Firing loading & marching with Gas Respirator on. AM3	
do	25/4/18		Route march 1 km. J shoot S.B.R.s were worn S.B.R.s worn for 2½ hrs. 20 Left 4 O.R.S. AM3	
do	26/4/18		Gas training. Aprl Lectures on Gas by Gde Gas Officer & Officers & S.O. O.R. 1 O.R. from M.G. Coy. Le Kiosk 2 O.R.S. AM3	
do	27/4/18		Gas training S.B.R.s worn for 2 hrs. Route march. To hosp 3 O.R.S. AM3	
do	28/4/18		Paraded at 20.30 and marched to NOYELLES and entrained at 03.15 — AM3 2	
LA LACQUE	29/4/18		Arrived in Camp at LA LACQUE at 13.10. 2 U.S. Amusage to half AM3	
do	30/4/18		Parade under Company arrangement Gas training. Lewis Gunner & Runners to hosp 3 O.R.S. Bow hosp 2 O.R.S. AM3	

2353 Wt. W2544/1454 700,000 5/15 D. D. & L. A.D.S.S./Forms/C. 2118.

WAR DIARY
or
INTELLIGENCE SUMMARY.

Army Form C. 2118.

Instructions regarding War Diaries and Intelligence Summaries are contained in F. S. Regs., Part II. and the Staff Manual respectively. Title pages will be prepared in manuscript.

(Erase heading not required.)

Summary of Events and Information

Summary of Casualties during April 1918.

Place	Date	Hour		Increase			Decrease			Remarks and references to Appendices
				Officers	O. Ranks	Total.	Officers	O. Ranks	Total.	
			From Hosps. wounded.	—	6	6	1	32	33	To Hosps. sick
			" " sick.	1	38	39	—	2	2	To I.B. Depot.
			Rejoined	1	7	8	—	6	6	To R.Y.C. (re commission)
			Reinforcements	—	3	3	—	12	12	Left in Egypt (Sick list)
			From 2nd L.H.A.	1	—	1	1	—	1	Rejoined 2nd L.H.A.
				3	54	57	2	52	54	
			Effective Strength. 46 Officers & 944 O. Ranks.							
			Ration Strength. 44 " 912 "							

Copy No. 10

1/7th. (Blythswood) Battalion   The Highland Light Infantry.

MOVE ORDERS NO. 7

By Lieut. Col. R. S. Gibbons, D.S.O., Commanding.   31/8/18

The 52nd. Division will take over the Battle Line at BULLECOURT from the 56th. Division.   The 157 Infantry Brigade will move to HENIN HILL AREA on 1st. September.

The Battalion will parade at 6.55 a.m. to-morrow, and will march off at 7 a.m.   Order of march : H.Qs., B, C, D, and A. Coys.

L.G. Limbers, cookers, water carts, officer's mess cart, and Maltese Cart will accompany Battalion.- Remainder of Transport will move under orders of Transport Officer to T.1.d.2.4. Sufficient ammunition to make up to 220 rounds per man will be sent up by limber to Bn. Bivouac area in the HINDENBURG LINE T.4.b. and T.5.a.   These ammunition limbers will then return to Transport Lines. All horses will be kept at Transport Lines.   Greatcoats will be packed in bundles by 6 a.m. and conveyed to new bivouac area by baggage wagons.   All other kits, officers valises, bivouac shelters etc. will be dumped at Q.M. Stores by 6.30 a.m.   Breakfast will be at 6 a.m.

From 7 p.m. to-night Battalion will be ready to move at 2 hours notice.

McWeir
Lieut. & A/Adjt.,
1/7th. Bn. H.L.I.

Distribution :-
1. A.Coy   7. Q.M.   13. 55th Bn
2. B. "   8. 139th Inf Bde.   14. File.
3. C. "   9. 137th : :   15.
4. D. "   10. 3rd Division.   16. War Diary.
5. T.O.   11. 46th Division.
6. Signals.   12. 55th Division.

SECRET. *Appendix I.* COPY NO. 12
2nd. April. 1918.

1/7th. (Blythswood) Battalion   The Highland Light Infantry.

BATTALION ORDER NO. 288.

By Lieut. Col. E. S. Gibbons, D.S.O., Commanding.

Ref. Map. PALESTINE. SHEET XIII

1. MOVE.
The 157th. Infantry Brigade Group will march from SARONA to SURAFEND CAMP (S.20b.) on the 3rd. April, 1918.
The head of the Column (5th. H.L.I.) will pass starting point at 1830.

2. STARTING POINT.
Light Railway Line at SARONA.

3. ROUTE.
Track running along left bank of NAHR EL BARIDEH. SHEIKH AMRAD (J.25), MAIN ROAD H.36.d.9.3.   Thence along RAMLEH - JAFFA Main Road.

4. PARADE.
The Battalion will parade at 1820 and will follow 6th. H.L.I. at 30 yards distance.
    Order of March.   Headquarters,
                       "A" Coy.
                       "B" Coy.
                       "C" Coy.
                       "D" Coy.

5. TRANSPORT.
Transport (except L.G. Pack Animals) will march in rear of the Battalion.
The strictest march discipline will be observed.
Field Cookers and Water Carts will be sent to new camp at 0900 on 3rd. instant.

6. ADVANCE PARTIES.
The following party will parade at 0600 on 3rd. instant, and will proceed to SURAFEND.
                Captain W. F. Todd
                Lieut. A. G. Clark
                4 Pioneers.
    Per Coy. and H.Qs. 1 N.C.O., 2 Cooks (1 per H.Q.), and 7 men
                        (one of whom will be a guide).
This party will be employed in laying out new area, for which purpose Pioneers will take ropes and sticks.
Cooks will prepare a hot meal to be ready on arrival of Battalion.
24 hours rations for this party will be drawn from SARONA Supply Dump at 1800 to-day.
Transport Officer will arrange transport for this party.

Major E. Watson, M.C., will meet the Staff Captain at Brigade Headquarters, SARONA, at 0730, on 3rd. inst., to proceed to SURAFEND, where camping ground will be pointed out.

7. SUPPLIES.
Supplies for consumption 3rd./4th. April will be drawn from SARONA Supply Dump at 0830 on 3rd. instant.

8. WATER.
            Drinking) SURAFEND Water Area.
            Watering) East of Camp.

                                        Capt. & Adjt.
                                        1/7th. Bn. H.L.I.

Copy No. 1. O.C. "A" Coy.
2. "B"
3. "C"
4. "D"
5. "H.Q."
6. Transport Officer.
7. Quarter-master.
8. Major Watson.
9. Captain Todd.
10. Office.
11. War Diary.
12. War Diary.

1/7TH. (Blythswood) Battalion   The Highland Light Infantry.
BATTALION ORDERS.
By Lieut. Col. E. S. Gibbons, D.S.O., Commanding.

SECRET.   28/4/18.

MOVE.   The Battalion (less "B" Coy.) will march to NOYELLES to-day and entrain for new area. Train leaves at 0314 on 29th. inst. Column will be formed up ready to pass starting point (Branch roads 700 yards S. of Church) at 2000. Signallers will parade with bicycles.   ORDER OF MARCH :-
          Scouts and Signallers,
          "A" Coy.
          "H.Q." Coy.
          "C" Coy.
          "D" Coy.
"B" Coy. will parade at 1145 and march to NOYELLES and proceed by first train leaving at 1814.

LOADING PARTY.   1 Officer and 50 Other Ranks detailed by O.C. "A" Coy will parade at 0945 and proceed to NOYELLES Railway Station to arrive there 3½ hours before departure of first train. This party will assist in loading trains previous to and including the Battalion train and will travel with Battalion. It will unload Bn. Baggage at detraining station.

ENTRAINING OFFICER.   Captain TODD will report to R.T.O., NOYELLES as Entraining Officer, 3 hours before departure of 1st. train. He will travel on the last train leaving entraining station at 1814 on 29th. inst.

TRANSPORT.   All Transport and animals will be at station 3½ hours before departure of train. 1 Cooker and team will go with "B" Coy. and accompany them on train. Q.M. will detail from ration party 1 man for each supply vehicle to act as guard. On arrival at new area these men will be attached to A.S.C. train till further orders.

REAR PARTY.   Each Coy. will detail 1 Officer and 12 men as a rear party to see that billets are left thoroughly clean and that no Government property is left behind. These parties will collect at starting point and follow the Battalion under the Senior Officer.
Rear party of B. Coy. will follow its own Company.

DISCIPLINE.   Standing Orders for trains will be strictly adhered to. No man will leave the train without permission. O.C. "C" and "D" Coys. will each detail a guard of 1 Officer and 12 men for the train journey. These guards will travel one at each end of the train, and at stations sentries will patrol each side of the train to ensure that orders are adhered to.

BAGGAGE AND TRANSPORT.   2 Limbered Wagons will be sent to each Coy. at 1700 to collect Officers' Kits, Lewis Guns and magazines. These will be taken to H.Q. Dump and loaded on train wagons. O.C. Coys. must send their Mess Baskets to H.Q. Mess by 1800. Transport is allotted as follows :-
  Each Coy. 1 Limbered G.S. Wagon for blankets   Total   5
            2   "   " Wagons for tools   2
            2   "   "   "   " S.B.R.Containers   2
            1   "   " Wagon for H.Q.Lewis Guns
                               and magazines   1

                                                            10

The limbers carrying blankets and S.B.R. Containers will be off loaded at station and loaded with S.A.A.
These blankets will be issued to Coys. and must then be carried by men. S.B.R. Containers will be loaded on the train.
Cooking pots, signalling equipment, orderly room boxes, and Coy. office office boxes will be taken to H.Q. Dump by 1800.

P.T.O.

(2)

Quarter-master and cooks will accompany the transport and have tea prepared for Bn. on arrival at Station.

                                                              Capt. & Adjt.,
                                           1/7th. Bn. H.L.I.

Copy No. 1.   O.C. "A" Coy.
         2   "B"
         3   "C"
         4   "D"
         5   "H.Q."
         6.   Q.M.
         7.   T.O.
         8.   Capt. Todd
         9   Office
        10   War Diary
        11   War Diary.

WAR DIARY
1/7th H.L.I.
1st - 31st MAY 1918

Volume III.

WAR DIARY or INTELLIGENCE SUMMARY

Army Form C. 2118.

Volume III
1/7th A.H.L.
1st to 31st May 1918

Place	Date	Hour	Summary of Events and Information	Remarks and references to Appendices
LA LACQUE	1/5/18		FRANCE Sheet 36. Gas training. Lewis Gun training + training of Runners by commanding officer round the manor line. Battery.	
do	2/5/18		Battery Lecture by Col Cockhill on "Use of the Regmnt. Coy training. Runners	
do	3/5/18		Company training. Lectures at AIRE to Officers on "Recent operations" at same time Gunners tried of men. So heft 1 OR. OMB	
do	4/5/18		Battalion marched to Cape Gas School where all the different methods of Gas attack were demonstrated also men were issued through Gas chambers in the field. MnB	
do	5/5/18		Church Parade	
do	6/5/18		Paraded at 07.00 marched to AIRE and entrained. Arrived at MAROEUIL where he billeted the night. OmB	
MAROEUIL	7/5/18		Paraded at 19.10 marched to VIMY RIDGE and took over from 87th CANADIAN Regt at about 08.30 following morning. So heft 10 ORs. Forces defenders hostile fell.	
VIMY	8/5/18		A few Gas shells and H.E. fell. Lt Miller and 7 ORs left thought air at 21.30 down Crows there are nightly lights tend about 6 + S.T ACHEVILLE RD and though it but there no sound of about six 0.15" burst 3m to left (2 bounds ? shell) Gas	
do	9/5/18		Very quiet all day only a few shells or shrapnel a Lewis Gun Clai shows have 20 HE at new trench at T.18.C.6.2 Gas 2 OR wounded to left. Gas	

WAR DIARY / INTELLIGENCE SUMMARY

Army Form C. 2118.

Volume XII
1/7th H.L.I.
1st to 31st May 1918

Place	Date	Hour	Summary of Events and Information	Remarks and references to Appendices
Vimy	10/5/18		Patrol of 1 N.C.O. and 6 men all MONTREAL TRENCH at ACHEVILLE RD to latest constantly between there and QUEBEC TRENCH along the northern side of the road. Enemy work seen at QUEBEC at 0300. They failed to reply to our artillery. Enemy trench mortars firing out in short bts all day. Our fire about 20 A.S. Shells. Enemy shelling hot G.A.h. 30.85 (1 wounded 22nd) arts. Sone shelling on Fort side. 2 Snipers Posts at Junction of TOT TRENCH. They	
do	11/5/18		claim 1 hit. Patrol 10 M/H + 5 OR M. VALLANCE and 5 OR off QUARRIES ROAD at check and harassed down it to junction with MERICOURT RD when they returned to left an hour, no enemy men seen or heard. 1 NCO + 6 patrolled from MONTREAL to junction of QUEBEC + TOT trenches. 1 OR who had been sent to see where they were returned at 0100, the remainder did not return till after dark having their man lay out in a shell hole all day. Guns 1 en + heavy trps. Enemy front machine guns at MONTREAL and also some light gas shells at NEW BRUNSWICK. During the day Some S/g shells or 4.2 in vicinity of QUEBEC trench.	
do	12/5/18		Patrol 2 Lt J.A. Falconer + 21 OR sent from Sun left T23.a.8.6 at 2230 to reconnoitre enemy wire round TEMPEST trench, on passing own 300 yds from MONTREAL trench Sergt + 1 man sent forward to investigate and signal 50-100 yds in advance of enemy line returned and out to be enemy last. Flares were sent up and M.G. fire opened. Patrol withdrawn with Officer + 3 OR wounded + 1 OR missing. 2/Lt McCormick 24 OR + Lewis Gun T10.d - 65.10. at 2300 to reconnoitre enemy wire	

Signed A.R. Howie ?

WAR DIARY
INTELLIGENCE SUMMARY

Army Form C. 2118.

17th H.L.I.   Volume III   1st to 31st May 1918

Place	Date	Hour	Summary of Events and Information	Remarks and references to Appendices
VIMY	12/5/18		On either side of MERICOURT Rd. at T.14.a.6.1. Officer and 2 ORs went forward to enemy wire but as listed on night our engaged and flares going up further front was intended so patrol returned at 0200. Which Lt. J.A. Palmer and 3 OR. Wounded. GW3	
do	13/5/18		Enemy artillery active during the night also a little shelling during the day. Own wire active. Patrol of Lt. G.W. Smith & Platoon wish Lewis Gun left 7.23.a.6.5 & 30 will orders to reconnoitre sap subtract from ABROAD Trench. Patrol had direction many to surprise being effected by enemy posts. Ours to shape 1 OR P.O.B.	
do	14/5/18		Artillery activity normal. At relief raid was carried out by C.O.C. & Lt. J.L. Kennedy Running Plateau Lt. Johnston and 1 Platoon B.C. Lt. Ritchie and Lt. Smith and at Hulse Alley. Stay out the two and forwarded the Hindenberg line about A BLAZE track for a while of about 60 yds were nor land for about 200 yds. No reliable information found. No of casualties 15 of HLI returned as first shot [...] & lay in No Mans land for some [...] hour of silence & lay in lined with us all subject any Batt in trench time of silence + coming to [...] H.Q. in VIMY. So lost 1 OR GW3	
do	15/5/18		Battalion in reserve at HQ allotted. Enemy art and own art active. GW3 2 OR1 (1 accidental shell) GW3	
do	16/5/18		A quiet day. A few gas shells at NC & the evening. We lost 1 OR. Gassed.	

Army Form C. 2118.

Instructions regarding War Diaries and Intelligence Summaries are contained in F. S. Regs., Part II. and the Staff Manual respectively. Title pages will be prepared in manuscript.

WAR DIARY
or
INTELLIGENCE SUMMARY.
(Erase heading not required.)

1/7th H.L.I. Volume III 1st to 31st May 1918

Place	Date	Hour	Summary of Events and Information	Remarks and references to Appendices
VIMY	17/5/18		Artillery normal. Work on defences. Losses 5 OR (2 wounded 2 sick) [illegible] 1 OR	AWB
do	18/5/18		Enemy Artillery active. Work on defences. Losses 5 OR. [illegible] 2 OR. AWB	
do	19/5/18		A very quiet day. Work continued. Losses 2 wounded & 1 sick. [illegible] 2 OR	AWB
do	20/5/18		Artillery normal. Work on defences. Lecture to B.G. [illegible] NCO Batt moved up at dusk and took over Bde right sector [illegible] FOREST from 1/5th HLI about 0100. Defensive patrols. Losses 8 OR. [illegible] 34 OR draft. AWB	
do	21/5/18		A quiet day but for some Blue Cross shells at night. [illegible] patrols. Capt R. J. [illegible] to hosp. AWB	
do	22/5/18		No activity. Patrol of 2nd Lieut [illegible] & 13 men reconnoitred [illegible] and WINNIPEG Roads and ground between. No enemy were seen. Losses 3 OR wounded & 1 sick. AWB	
do	23/5/18		Enemy Artillery fairly active. A patrol Lt Wylie + 16 ORs with Lewis Gun left TWELFTH AV at 2200 and proceeded to T.17.b.7.3. From here Officer & 2 OR scouts pushed forward to T.18.a.3.6 where a disused enemy post was found. Owing to flares no further progress was made. Patrol returned at 0200. Sick 1 OR	AWB
do	24/5/18		A quiet day. 1500 cylinders Gas "Beam" was successfully launched against enemy	[illegible]

2353 Wt. W2544/1454 700,000 5/15 D. D. & L. A.D.S.S./Forms/C. 2118.

Army Form C. 2118.

WAR DIARY
or
INTELLIGENCE SUMMARY.
(Erase heading not required.)

Volume VII
1/7th A.L.I.
1st to 31st May 1918.

Place	Date	Hour	Summary of Events and Information	Remarks and references to Appendices
VIMY	1/5/18		On our relief by 32nd R.F. returned to our old line bivouac area at 9.30 when relieved.	
ST ELOY	2/5/18		Left marched to St Eloy arriving country billets about 0300 on 2/5/18.	
do	28/5/18		Spent 5 on Training and Tactical Training. All ranks were in camp. About 0315 am enemy fired from 15 to 20 rounds on our camp from M.G. in aeroplane. No casualties.	
do	29/5/18		Day spent cleaning up & kit 2nd line gear.	
do	29/5/18		Normal Training. Reception of draft & Coy Commander gave lect 2 on Scheme 47. Y. O. R. to commence tomorrow.	
do	30/5/18		Classes of Company training, Lewis, Company Schemes Rifle Grenade, bombing 3 in Scheme Lect 8 CAMB given on long bus of enemy man to included Battery. Lect on 27 M.B. 1st 2nd Bns & Coys of CAMB & Lewis Range heed being town in dry toasty and air in Rifles General instruction. Lect 303 On SSS on M.G. from fraging battery and known enemy MGs. batnd.	
do	31/5/18		Rigging battery cards. Mounts round for stalk 2nd O.C. in Lewis Gun Range. (Ban.)	

Effective strength 46 Officers & 944 O. Ranks. On 1st May 1918.
Ration " 44 " & 912 "

D.W. [signature]

Army Form C. 2118.

WAR DIARY
or
INTELLIGENCE SUMMARY.

(Erase heading not required.)

Volume III
1st to 31st May 1918

Summary of Events and Information

Summary of Casualties for May 1918.

	Officers	O.Ranks	Total		Officers	O.Ranks	Total
From Hospital Wounded	—	1	1	To Hospital Wounded	1	20	21
" " Sick	1	9	9	" " Sick	2	76	78
				Missing	—	1	1
Rejoined	—	34	34	Taken Prisoners	1	2	2
				To L.I. in Batty	1	1	1
				To W.K. ne Commissn	1	1	1
Total	—	44	44	Total	3	101	104

Effective Strength 43 Officers & 899 O.Ranks
Ration " 29 " & 724 "

1/7th. (Blythswood) Battalion   The Highland Light Infantry.

BATTALION ORDERS.

By Lieut. Col. E. S. Gibbons, D.S.O., Commanding.

5/5/18.

<u>MOVE.</u>

Battalion will parade at 0700, and march to AIRE to entrain at 0808.

<u>Dress</u> :- Marching order, waterproof sheets and steel helmets on packs.

All Officers' kits, cooking pots, medical equipment, blankets and any other baggage will be stacked on Battalion parade ground by 0545.

O.C. Coys. will detail a loading party of 4 men each to load lorry at 0600.   O.C. "D" Coy. will detail officer to superintend.

Reveille will be at 0430.
Breakfast will be at 0500.

M.O. will detail unfit men to go on lorry to station under officer detailed above.

[signature]
Capt. & Adjt.,
1/7th. Bn. H.L.I.

1/7th. (Blythswood) Battalion The Highland Light Infantry.
BATTALION ORDER.

By Lieut. Col. E. S. Gibbons, D.S.O., Commanding.

5/5/18

MOVE.

Battalion will parade at 0700, and march to AIRE to entrain at 0808.

Dress :- Marching order, waterproof sheets and steel helmets on packs.

All Officers' kits, cooking pots, medical equipment, blankets, and any other baggage, will be stacked on Battalion parade ground by 0545.

O.C. Coys. will detail a loading party of 4 men each to load lorry at 0600. O.C. "D" Coy. will detail officer to superintend.

Reveille will be at 0430.
Breakfast will be at 0500.

M.O. will detail unfit men to go on lorry to station, under officer detailed above.

Capt. & Adjt.,
1/7th. Bn. H.L.I.

SECRET.   Copy No. 9

A raiding party under Lieut. KELMAN will carry out a raid to-night on enemy's lines.
Party :   1 Platoon B. Coy. under 2/Lieut. JOHNSTON. *Raiding platoon*
            1 Platoon C. Coy. under 2/Lieut. WALKER. *Supporting platoon*
Covering party : 2 Platoon of B. Coy. will take 2 Lewis Guns.
                 Platoon of C. Coy. will take 1 Lewis Gun.
The point to be raided will be T.19 C OY. 40, 50 yards South of ABLAZE trench, and the object of the raid is :
     (a) to obtain identification,
     (b) to inflict casualties.
Raiding party will not stop for (b) when once (a) has been obtained.
Starting point will be TWELFTH AVENUE - bearing to object 43° T distance 200 yds.
Live prisoners are required and anything which will establish identity of unit opposite, such should be brought away, such as enemy shoulder straps, packs etc.   Officers, N.C.Os. and men taking part in the raid will not carry any letters, papers, pay books, or identity discs, regimental badges or buttons etc. which would lead to identification.
The actual raid will take place at a hour to be notified later. Raiding party will leave starting point in sufficient time to gain a position of assembly in "No Man's Land" as close to enemy's wire as possible whence the raid can be launched at the hour ordered.
At dusk a tape will be laid out from starting point to show line of direction and 4 men stationed along it.
Scouts in front of the raiding platoon will cut the wire and after platoon has passed through will improve the gaps for return journey.
As soon as wire is cut the sections detailed will proceed to their tasks :- 1 section with Lewis Gun will rush a possible post at head of ABLAZE C.T. and establish a block NORTH of it in enemy's outpost line.
1 section will rush straight across outpost trench and then half-left to ABLAZE TRENCH, where it will establish a block, the remainder of the section clearing trench westward to head of trench. 1 section with Lewis Gun will rush from wire gap half-right and establish a block in enemy outpost trench.   The remaining section will rush straight into outpost trench and work outwards towards section on right and to head of ABLAZE TRENCH.
O.C. raiding platoon with 2 men will be in outpost trench in front of wire gap -
O.C. raiding party where he can best control operations.
The supporting platoon will cover the operations against attack from outside and will cover the withdrawal of raiding platoon.
Stretcher bearers will be with support platoon.
Party will withdraw as soon as identification has been taken. Signal for withdrawal will be 2 G's on bugle.
Party will return to TWELFTH AVENUE and on reaching our line will report at once to Bn. Hqrs.
                              P.T.O.

(2)

Dress :- bandolier
Rifle, bayonet, S.B.As. in alert position. Each man will carry four bombs. One section of supporting platoon will take rifle grenades.

The raid will be carried out silently with the bayonet only, unless circumstances demand otherwise.

Password :- BULLY.

[signature]
Capt. & Adjt.,
1/7th. Bn. H.L.I.
14/8/16.

Copy No. 1. O.C. "B" Coy.
2. O.C. "C" Coy.
3. Lt. Kelman.
4. G.O.C., 157 Inf. Bde.
5. O.C., 1/4th. K.O.S.B.
6. O.C., 1/5th. H.L.I.
7. C.O.
8. War Diary.
9. War Diary.

1/7th. (Blythswood) Battalion   The Highland Light Infantry Copy no 6
B A T T A L I O N   O R D E R S.
Secret   By Lieut. Col. E. S. Gibbons, D.S.O., Commanding.   14/5/18

The Battalion will be relieved in this sectors by the 5th. H.L.I. on the night of 14/15th. May 1918.

A. Coy. 5th. H.L.I. will relieve A. Coy. 7th. H.L.I.
B. Coy.   do.   do.   B. Coy.   do.
C. Coy.   do.   do.   C. Coy.   do.
D. Coy.   do.   do.   D. Coy.   do.

On relief Coys. will proceed to sector vacated by 5th. H.L.I. and will take over areas previously occupied by similar lettered Coys. of 5th. H.L.I.

5th. H.L.I. will move up to the line by the undernoted routes and Coys. of 7th. H.L.I. will proceed to their areas by the reverse routes :-

A. Coy. by CANADA TRENCH - PEGGIE C.T. - TEDDIE GERARD.
B. Coy. by MERICOURT ROAD - NOVA SCOTIA ROAD - CANADA TRENCH - TOAST - MCDERMID - TUNNEL.
C. Coy. by MERICOURT ROAD - NOVA SCOTIA ROAD - CANADA TRENCH - TOAST C.T..
D. Coy. by MERICOURT ROAD to TEDDIE GERARD.
H.Qs.Coy by PEGGIE C.T. - CANADA TRENCH - TOAST - MCDERMID TRENCH.

Guides 1 per platoon will meet Coys. of 5th. H.L.I. at following places :-

A. Coy. - Junction PEGGIE and CANADA trenches.
B. Coy. - Junction CANADA TRENCH and TOAST TRENCH.
C. Coy. -   do.   and   do.
D. Coy. - Junction of MERICOURT ROAD and HULL ROAD.
H.Qs.Coy - Junction of CANADA and TOAST TRENCHES.

Guides of 5th. H.L.I. will remain at these points and conduct Coys. of 7th. H.L.I. to their areas.

All trench stores, ammunition, bombs, rifle grenades etc. will be handed over.

Coys. will report completion of relief by codeword. to Bn Hqrs

Lewis guns and magazines will be carried by Coys.

Cooking pots, signalling equipment, medical panniers, and orderly room box will be at Bn. Hqrs. by 2100, and will be taken by carrying parties detailed by S.M. to where transport will be waiting T 21 a. 6.0.

The following will proceed to new area at 1000 to-day to take over stores etc. :

per platoon - 1 N.C.O.
H.Qrs. - 2/Lt. Sandeman, 4 Other Ranks.
1 N.C.O. and 5 signallers.

Capt. & Adjt.
1/7th. H.L.I.

S E C R E T.
1/7th. (Blythswood) Battalion   The Highland Light Infantry.
              B A T T A L I O N   O R D E R S.

By Lieut. Col. E. S. Gibbons, D.S.O., Commanding.   19/5/18.
_____

RELIEF.
The Battalion will relieve the 5th. H.L.I. in the front line on the night of the 20th./21st. May, 1918, in the following order :
"D" Coy. will take over from "B" Coy. 5th. H.L.I. :-
1st. Line from ACHEVILLE ROAD (exclusive) to junction of LIDSETT and QUEBEC (exclusive) with posts in TOT and TWELFTH AVENUE.
Main line from ACHEVILLE ROAD (exclusive) to L L in BRUNSWICK. Communication between Main Line and 1st. Line via TEASER and TOPER.

"A" Coy. will take over from "C" Coy. 5th. H.L.I. :-
1st. Line from junction LIDSETT and QUEBEC (inclusive) to QUARRIES ROAD (inclusive) with posts in TORQUAY.
Main Line from L L in BRUNSWICK to TOAST (exclusive).
Communication via TOAST and QUEBEC.

"B" Coy. will take over from "D" Coy. 5th. H.L.I. :-
1st. Line from QUARRIES ROAD (exclusive) to MERICOURT ROAD (inclusive) with post in TOAST.
Main Line from TOAST (inclusive) to MERICOURT ROAD (inclusive).
Communication via TOAST.

"C" Coy. will take over from "A" Coy. 5th. H.L.I. :-
1st. Line and Main Line from MERICOURT ROAD (exclusive) to VESTA TILLEY (exclusive).
Post in TOLEDO on HULL ROAD.

        Move will take place after dark by following routes :
"D" Coy. via GRAND TRUNK and TOAST.
"A" Coy. via TOAST (to move up after "D" Coy.)
"B" Coy. via PEGGIE and TEDDIE GERARD.
"C" Coy. via PEGGIE and TEDDIE GERARD (to move up after "B" Coy.).
"H.Qs" Coy. via GRAND TRUNK, TOAST, MCDERMID.

Company Commanders and 1 N.C.O. per platoon will go up to line this afternoon to see dispositions.
Signalling Officer, and 4 signallers, Scouts Officer and 3 observers, Gas N.C.O. and 2 N.C.O. per platoon and H.Qrs. will go up to line tomorrow at 1000.
H.Qrs. and Platoon N.C.Os. will take over all area and trench stores etc.

Trench Stores, communications, R.E. and Area Stores, Trench diagrams and defence schemes will be taken over. All Lewis Guns and Magazines will be carried up.
Completion of relief will be reported to Bn. Hqrs. by CODE.

                                         Capt. & Adjt.,
                                         1/7th. Bn. H. L. I.

Copy No. 1.   O.C. "A" Coy.
         2.   "B"
         3.   "C"
         4.   "D"
         5.   "H.Qrs."
         6.   5th. H.L.I.
         7.   C.O.
         8 and 9. War Diary.

SECRET.   Copy No.
1/7th. (Blythswood) Battalion   The Highland Light Infantry.
          BATTALION   ORDERS.
    By Lieut. Col. E. S. Gibbons, D.S.O., Commanding.
                                                        19/5/18.

RELIEF.
    The Battalion will relieve the 5th. H.L.I. in the front line on
the night of the 20th./21st. May, 1918, in the following order :
"D" Coy. will take over from "B" Coy. 5th. H.L.I. :-
    1st. Line from ACHEVILLE ROAD (exclusive) to junction of
    LIDSETT and QUEBEC (exclusive) with posts in TOT and TWELFTH
    AVENUE.
    Main line from ACHEVILLE ROAD (exclusive) to L L in
    BRUNSWICK.   Communication between Main Line and 1st. line
    via TEASER and TOPER.

"A" Coy. will take over from "C" Coy. 5th. H.L.I. :-
    1st. Line from junction LIDSETT and QUEBEC (exclusive) to
    QUARRIES ROAD (inclusive) with posts in TORQUAY.
    Main Line from L L in BRUNSWICK to TOAST (exclusive).
    Communication via TOAST and QUEBEC.

"B" Coy. will take over from "D" Coy. 5th. H.L.I. :-
    1st. Line from QUARRIES ROAD (exclusive) to MERICOURT ROAD
    (inclusive) with post in TOAST.
    Main line from TOAST (inclusive) to MERICOURT ROAD (inclusive).
    Communication via TOAST.

"C" Coy. will take over from "A" Coy. 5th. H.L.I. :-
    1st. Line and Main Line from MERICOURT ROAD (exclusive) to
    VESTA TILLEY (exclusive).
    Post in TOLEDO on HULL ROAD.

            Move will take place after dark by following routes :
    "D" Coy. via GRAND TRUNK and TOAST.
    "A" Coy. via TOAST (to move up after "D" Coy.)
    "B" Coy. via PUGGIE and TEDDIE GERARD.
    "C" Coy. via PUGGIE and TEDDIE GERARD (to move up after "B"
                                                        Coy.).
    "H.Qs" Coy. via GRAND TRUNK, TOAST, MCDERMID.

Company Commanders and 1 N.C.O. per platoon will go up to line this
afternoon to see dispositions.
Signalling Officer, and 4 signallers , Scouts Officer and 3
observers, Gas N.C.O. and 1 N.C.O. per platoon and H.Qrs. will
go up to line tomorrow at 1000.
H.Qrs. and Platoon N.C.Os. will take over all area and trench
stores etc.

Trench Stores, communications, R.E. and Area Stores, Trench
diagrams and defence schemes will be taken over.   All Lewis
Guns and Magazines will be carried up.
Completion of relief will be reported to Bn. Hqrs. by CODE.

                                            Capt. & Adjt.,
                                            1/7th. Bn. H.L.I.

Copy No. 1.   O.C. "A" Coy.
       2.   "B"
       3.   "C"
       4.   "D"
       5.   "H.Qrs."
       6.   5th. H.L.I.
       7.   C.O.
       8 and 9.   War Diary.

SECRET. COPY NO. 10.
1/7th. (Blythswood) Battalion   The Highland Light Infantry.

BATTALION ORDERS.

By Lieut. Col. E. S. Gibbons, D.S.O., Commanding.   23/5/18

---

1. The Battalion will be relieved in the line by the 5th. R.S.F. on the night of 24th./25th. May 1918, and after relief will take over billets of 5th. R.S.F. in OTTAWA CAMP, MONT ST. ELOY.
   Coys. will be relieved as follows :-
   "A" Coy. by "C" Coy. 5th. R.S.F.
   "B" Coy. by "B" Coy.   do.
   "C" Coy. by "A" Coy.   do.
   "D" Coy. by "D" Coy.   do.

2. Guides (1 Officer per Coy., 1 O.R. per platoon, 1 Officer and 3 O.Rs. per Headquarters) will meet the relieving Bn. at the Barrier on the LA FOLIE - NEUVILLE ST. VAAST ROAD at 2030 on the 24th. inst. and will conduct Coys. and platoons up to the line. "D", "C", "H.Qs" "A" Coys. 5th. R.S.F. in order named by route VIMY - GRAND TRUNK TRENCH - TOAST.
   "B" Coy. R.S.F. by HUMBER TRENCH - PEGGY C.T.   The 4th. R.S.F. relieving 5th. A.& S.H. have precedence of roads.
   Coy. Officers will march their own guides down.
   In the event of an alarm during relief, troops will halt and send an officer to report at H.Qs. of the Bn. in whose area they happen to be.
   Communications, trench maps, defence schemes, log books, Soyers' stoves, food containers, petrol tins, and all trench and area stores will be handed over on relief and receipts obtained.
   The extra day's rations now on hand will be handed over to relieving Battalion.

3. After relief Coys. will proceed by platoons to the barrier on the LA FOLIE - NEUVILLE ST. VAAST ROAD by same route as relieving Coys. come up, and will be conveyed to billeting areas by motor buses or lorries.   Each bus will hold one platoon.   Lieut. MUIR and Staff Captain will be embussing officers and will allocate buses. Parties will be drawn up on right of road facing direction in which convoy is proceeding.   Men must get into buses quickly, when ordered to do so.

4. O.C. Details will send billeting parties of 1 Officer per Coy. and 1 N.C.O. or reliable private per platoon (1 Officer and 4 O.Rs. for Bn. Hs) to Bn. Billeting area on morning of 24th. instant.
   These parties will meet platoons etc. on arrival and conduct them to billets.
   Personnel from Training Camp will rejoin Bn. in billeting area and must be at MONT ST. ELOY by 1800 on 24th. inst.
   Transport will move from present lines to lines occupied by relieving battalion.   Relief to be completed by 1400 on 24th. inst.

5. In case of approach of hostile aircraft during move party will clear off roads and remain still until danger is past.

6. Completion of relief will be reported by O.C. Coys. by CODE to Bn. Hs.   Arrival in billets will be reported to Bn. Hs.

7. Baths at ST. ELOY are allotted as under on 25th. inst:-
   0800 - 0930 "A" Coy.;   0930 - 1100 "B" Coy.;   1100 - 1200 "C" -
   1300 - 1330 "C" & 1330 - 1500 "D" ;- 1500 - 1630 "H.Qs"
   Accomodation - 50 men per half-hour.

Capt. & Adjt.
1/7th. Bn. H.L.I.

Copy No. 1. O.C. "A" Coy.
         2.   "B"
         3.   "C"
         4.   "D"
         5.   "H.Q"
         6. Q.M.
         7. T.O.
         8. C.O.
         9. O.C., Details.
         10 and 11. War Diary.

SECRET.   COPY NO. /1

1/7th. (Blythswood) Battalion   The Highland Light Infantry.

BATTALION ORDERS.

By Lieut. Col. E. S. Gibbons, D.S.O., Commanding.

---

1. The Battalion will be relieved in the line by the 5th. R.S.F. on the night of 24th./25th. May 1918, and after relief will take over billets of 5th. R.S.F. in OTTAWA CAMP, MONT ST. ELOY.
   Coys. will be relieved as follows :-
   "A" Coy. by "C" Coy. 5th. R.S.F.
   "B" Coy. by "B" Coy.   do.
   "C" Coy. by "A" Coy.   do.
   "D" Coy. by "D" Coy.   do.

2. Guides (1 Officer per Coy., 1 O.R. per platoon, 1 Officer and 3 O.Rs. per Headquarters) will meet the relieving Bn. at the Barrier on the LA FOLIE - NEUVILLE ST. VAAST ROAD at 2030 on the 24th. inst. and will conduct Coys. and platoons up to the line. "D", "C", "H.Qs" "A" Coys. 5th. R.S.F. in order named by route VIMY - GRAND TRUNK TRENCH - TOAST.
   "B" Coy. R.S.F. by HUMBER TRENCH - PEGGY C.T.   The 4th. R.S.F. relieving 5th. A. & S.H. have precedence of roads.
   Coy. Officers will march their own guides down.
   In the event of an alarm during relief, troops will halt and send an officer to report at H.Qs. of the Bn. in whose area they happen to be.
   Communications, trench maps, defence schemes, log books, Soyers' stoves, food containers, petrol tins, and all trench and area stores will be handed over on relief and receipts obtained.
   The extra day's rations now on hand will be handed over to relieving Battalion.

3. After relief Coys. will proceed by platoons to the barrier on the LA FOLIE - NEUVILLE ST. VAAST ROAD by same route as relieving Coys. come up, and will be conveyed to billeting areas by motor buses or lorries.   Each bus will hold one platoon.   Lieut. MUIR and Staff Captain will be embussing officers and will allocate buses.   Parties will be drawn up on right of road facing direction in which convoy is proceeding.   Men must get into buses quickly, when ordered to do so.

4. O.C. Details will send billeting parties of 1 Officer per Coy. and 1 N.C.O. or reliable private per platoon (1 Officer and 4 O.Rs. for Bn. Hs) to Bn. Billeting area on morning of 24th. instant. These parties will meet platoons etc. on arrival and conduct them to billets.
   Personnel from Training Camp will rejoin Bn. in billeting area and must be at MONT ST. ELOY by 1800 on 24th. inst.
   Transport will move from present lines to lines occupied by relieving battalion.   Relief to be completed by 1400 on 24th. inst.

5. In case of approach of hostile aircraft during move party will clear off roads and remain still until danger is past.

6. Completion of relief will be reported by O.C. Coys. by CODE to Bn. Hs.   Arrival in billets will be reported to Bn. Hs.

7. Baths at ST. ELOY are allotted as under on 25th. inst:-
   0800 - 0930 "A" Coy.: 0930 - 1100 "B" Coy.: 1100 - 1200 "C" -
   1300 - 1330 "C" + 1330 - 1500 "D" : 1500 - 1630 "H.Qs"
   Accomodation - 50 men per half-hour.

                                                    Capt. & Adjt.
                                                    1/7th. Bn. H.L.I.

Copy No. 1.   O.C. "A" Coy.
        2.   "B"
        3.   "C"
        4.   "D"
        5.   "H.Q"
        6.   Q.M.
        7.   T.O.
        8.   C.O.
        9.   O.C., Details.
        10 and 11.   War Diary.

d. I
13 sheets

Vol 3

Capt AHR

War Diary - June - 1915

WAR DIARY
INTELLIGENCE SUMMARY

Army Form C. 2118.

1/4th H.L.I.

Volume III
1st to 30th June 1918

Place	Date	Hour	Summary of Events and Information	Remarks and references to Appendices
ST. ELOY	1/6/18		Effective strength 46 Officers & 944 O'Ranks.	
do	1/6/18		Ration " 44 " 912 " "	
do	2/6/18		Digging - protection for huts - touch coy on known extensive wiring. YB	
			Battalion relieved the 4th CR in the Right Reserve of the WILLERVAL Section of the Divisional Sector - Left camp at ST. ELOY at 1315 and took over new area about 1800. Major E. Watson M.B. in command. L.Col J. Hayes and the nucleus proceeded from ST. ELOY to RISPIN CAMP, VILLERS AU BOIS Schoof 4 OR. sick YB	
WILLERVAL SECTION	3/6/18		Quiet day. - From hosp 1 OR. Schoof 6 OR sick. YB	
do	4/6/18		Enemy shelled features near our trenches fairly heavily in the morning - otherwise quiet. From hosp. 1 OR. Schoof 2 OR sick. YB	
do	5/6/18		Some trenches again shelled in the morning and at 9.45pm - kept trench min. with work on the trenches. Schoof 6 O.R. sick. YB	
do	6/6/18		Artillery normal. - work on trenches continued. From hosp 1 OR Schoof 3 OR. sick. YB	
d.o.	7/6/18		Abt 100 Blue Cross shells fell on battalion area. Otherwise day quiet. Work on trenches continued. From hospital 1 OR. 2 Schoof 5 OR sick. YB	
do	8/6/18		Day very quiet. Battalion moved into support line relieved 1/5 H.L.I. in Right Section WILLERVAL Section by daylight Relief carried by 1700. 2 Schoof 1 OR 1/6 A Pilcocken 4 OR sick, 11 OR wounded YB	
do	9/6/18		System of defence reorganised - support line converted into main line of resistance. From hosp 1 OR Schoof 1 OR wounded 3 OR sick. YB	
do	10/6/18		Artillery normal. Patrol 2 OR. IC OR 1 OR T 28 A + 3 at 2300 and reconnoitred enemy's front on ANTELOPE ALLEY returning at 0200. Patrol 2 I.O. 2 OR reconnoitred No Man's Land. From hosp. 1 OR Schoof 2 OR sick. YB and 1 BG sick, 2 OR wounded YB	
do	11/6/18		Quiet day. All available working parties at night on wiring. From hosp. 1 OR Schoof 2 NCO sick YB. Patrol of 1 NCO and 3 OR from centre of	
do	12/6/18		4th S.O.S. started from centre Coy 0122 - firing continued by night 0300. Schoof 3 OR sick. YB reconnoitred No Mans Land from 2300 - 0300	

WAR DIARY
or
INTELLIGENCE SUMMARY.
(Erase heading not required)

Army Form C. 2118.

Volume III
1st to 30th June 1918.

1/4th H.L.I.

Place	Date	Hour	Summary of Events and Information	Remarks and references to Appendices
WILLERVAL SECTION	13/6/18		Quiet day. wiring continued by night. Patrol encountered & dispersed an enemy patrol of 2/Lt W.P. Mackie and 10 O.R. met 1/Lt B. and 5 O.R. at 2300. approached along TIRED ALLEY to supper occupied post at B.S.C.4.9. then ourselves was dropped by our enemy wire. enemy's forward post put up by 7 O.R. from Mine camp. Enemy post was broken by a fine running from it. Having thrown a number of bombs into hostile patrol withdrew. From hof 1 O.R. Sholl 2 O.R. sick.	
do.	14/6/18		Artillery quiet. Battalion returned on YUKON AREA by 5th H.L.I. taking over FARBUS AREA from 5th H.L.I. which completed by daylight. Work on BROWN LINE was at night. From hof. 2 O.R. Sholl 3 O.R. sick.	
do.	15/6/18		Day normal - all available attention still given to wiring - From hof. Sholl ml.Ya.	
do.	16/6/18		Day normal. From hof. 2 O.R. draft 17 Sholl 2 sick Ya.	
do.	17/6/18		Shot enemy shoots on THELUS and FARBUS - Practice in contact aeroplane work was carried out from Bn HQ. hill room. Sholl 1 O.R. wounded. 1 O.R. sick 2/Lt H.N. Pelam to U.K. (on g.Ferrainy centre Yantham) Ya.	
do.	18/6/18		Day normal. enemy quiet at day. From hof. 2 O.R. draft. 5 Sholl. 1 O.R. wounded 3 O.R. sick Ya.	
do.	19/6/18		Day quiet - work on wire continued. From hof. 1 O.R. Sholl ml.Ya.	
do.	20/6/18		Battalion relieved in FARBUS AREA by 5th K.O.S.B. and proceeded by motor bus to OTTAWA camp ST. ELOY - settled down in new camp by 1900 ? From hof. 3 O.R. draft 1 Sholl 4 O.R. U.K. Ya.	
ST. ELOY	21/6/18		Day spent in cleaning up - each coy had 2 hours at the baths. Ten officers attended a Tank demonstration at WAYRANS. From hof O.1 O.R. Sholl 5 O.R. sick 2 Pvt. 3 O.R. to Edinburgh 1 O.R. Ya.	
do.	22/6/18		A & B Coys at the range. C & D coys 3 hours coy training. 2 hospital 2 O.R. sick Ya.	
do.	23/6/18		Battalion on duty on the Rhe - supplied 2 working parties of 60 men, guards forgents to in ST. ELOY - Church parade on Y.M.C.A. hut at 1000 . From hof 9 O.R. from A.S.C. 1 O.R. from Tractors in right. 1 O.R. Sholl. 1 O.R. sick. Ya.	
do.	24/6/18		20 men per coy m.t.g. ranges nee L.F.O. 3 hours specialist coy training - School for junior N.C.O.s started. 4 hours hof. Boyd. To hosp. H.O.R. Sick Ya.	

Army Form C. 2118.

WAR DIARY or INTELLIGENCE SUMMARY.

(Erase heading not required.)

Volume III
1st to 30th June 1918.

1/4th A.L.I.

Place	Date	Hour	Summary of Events and Information	Remarks and references to Appendices
ST. ELOY	25/6/18		N.C.Os Class under Capt. Boyd. - remainder occupied with 3 hours digging round huts. From hosp. 2 OR. To hosp. 5 OR. Sick 9/8.	
do	26/6/18		Battalion on Bde. duties. N.C.O. class continued for remainder - digging protection for huts. From hosp. 1 OR. To hosp. 2 OR. Sick 9/8.	
do	27/6/18		9 am to 12 am N.C.O. class. For remainder three hours digging round huts. 2 hm. to 6 hm. Bde Sports at LANCASTER CAMP. From hosp. 1 OR, to hosp. 2 OR. Taken on strength 2/Lt T.M.B. 1 officer. 2/Lt. A.N. Vallance and 1 OR 9/8.	
do	28/6/18		Battalion on Brigade Duties - whole battalion employed on Generals or working parties. From hosp. 1 officer (/Lt. Col. B.J. Gibson) and 1 OR. To hosp. 6 OR sick 9/8.	
VIMY	29/6/18		Battalion relieved 4th R.S. on front line night subsection Chaudiere section - moved off from ST. ELOY by motor lorries starting to embus at 9 am. Relief completed by 4 pm. Nucleus under Major E. Watson M.C. moved to RISPIN CAMP. VILLERS AU BOIS. From hosp. 1 OR. To hosp. 6 OR. sick 9/8.	
do	30/6/18		Very quiet day. Patrol of 2 officers (2/Lt N.G. Wilson and N.E. Prosser U.S.R.) left T.17.B.1.2 at 10.50 p.m. and reconnoitred enemy ad/ heads at T.18.a.4.4. Patrol of three officers 2/Lt Griffith and 1 L.G. section left T.16.b.5.1. at 10.45 hours proceed to T.11.a.6.2. Where enemy post had previously been located. The post was found but there were no signs of recent occupation. To hosp. 1 OR wounded, 1 officer (2/Lt W.P. Mackay) and 4 O.R. sick 9/8	

Army Form C. 2118.

WAR DIARY
or
INTELLIGENCE SUMMARY.
(Erase heading not required)

1/4th Batt. Volunteer III
1st to 30 June - 1918.

Place	Date	Hour	Summary of Events and Information							Remarks and references to Appendices
			Summary of Casualties for June - 1918.							
			Increase —	Officers	o'Ranks	Total	Decrease —	Officers	o'Ranks	Total
			From Hospitals – Wounded	-	1	1	To Hospitals – Wounded	-	10	10
[x Lieut J Bond S			Do. Do. – Sick	1	34	35	Do. Do. – Sick	3*	23	26
Z.S. Gibbons D.S.O.			Drafts from Base	-	24	24	To Mov. Emr. Traing. Estab. Zeitoun	1#	1	2
			Rejoined from hosp. last 18 in Egypt	-	1	1	To Base for Classification	-	3	3
							Do. Corps as Instrument.	-	1	1
							Taken on Strength of E.T.M.B.	1*	1	2
				1	60	61		5	98	23

Effective Strength – 40 Officers x 834 o'Ranks
Ration Strength – 27 Do x 678 Do

* 2 Lts. L.S. Gibbons D.S.O.
  Capt. P.S. Falconer
  2/Lt W.P. Marshall
2 Lieut. H.W. Roberts
o 2 Lt. H.W. Redwood.

SECRET.   Copy No. 10

1/7th. (Blythswood) Battalion   The Highland Light Infantry.

BATTALION ORDERS.

By Lieut. Col. E. S. Gibbons, D.S.O., Commanding.   1/6/18

Reference Map MAROEUIL. 1/20,000.

1. The Battalion will relieve the 7th. Bn. S. R. in Right Reserve in the Right (WILLERVAL) Section of the Divisional Sector on the 2nd. June.

       Coys. will relieve as follows :-
       "A" Coy. 7th. H.L.I. will relieve 7th. S.R. "A" Coy.
       "B" Coy.   do   do.   do.   "D" Coy.
       "C" Coy.   do.   do.   do.   "C" Coy.
       "D" Coy.   do.   do.   do.   "B" Coy.

2. The Boundaries of the WILLERVAL Section are as follows :-
    Right Boundary - TIRED ALLEY - SPUR POST (B 14 c central) - BORDER POST (B 13 a) all inclusive.
    Subsection boundary - WESTERN ROAD (inclusive to Right subsection).
    Left boundary - ACHEVILLE - NEW BRUNSWICK ROAD (both inclusive) as far as junction of GRAND TRUNK with BROWN LINE (exclusive), thence to CEMETERY (T 25 d 6. 9.) inclusive, thence to BOIS DU GOUCOT at T 25 c 00. 00. and thence due W. along the GRID Line.

3. Advance parties as under will go into the line on the 1st. June :
    2/Lieut. WEIR and 4 observers.   1 N.C.O. and 4 O.Rs. (1 per platoon) per Coy. to be at 156 Bde. Hqrs. at 1400.
    Bn. Signalling Officer and Signallers as detailed.

4. The Bn. will proceed in Motor Buses to debussing point on NEUVILLE ST. VAAST - THELUS ROAD, about 1000 yards W. of LES TILLEUS cross roads.
    All movement East of NEUVILLE ST. VAAST will be by sections at 100 to 150 yards distance.
    7th. S. R. are providing two chains of picquets.
    Upper chain - from debussing point to W. end of MERSEY ALLEY
                   (avoiding Canadian Monument)
    Lower chain - from debussing point to junction of TIRED ALLEY
               and THELUS RIDGE Line. (avoiding Canadian Monument)
    Forward of these points guides will be arranged.

    B. and C. Coys. will proceed by Lower Chain.
    A. and D. Coys. and Hqrs. will proceed by Upper Chain and MERSEY ALLEY.

The Post of "C" Coy. to be located in VANCOUVER ROAD cannot carry out relief till after dark, and till then will be retained in POST LINE.

        All S.O.S. Posts must be taken over.
8 Lewis Guns and 1 Lewis Gun for A.A. per Coy. will be taken up, except that "A" Coy. will leave 1 Lewis Gun with details.
A supply of 28 magazines per gun (16 per A.A. gun) will be

P.T.O.

(2)

maintained. These with the exception of 10 magazines per gun which will be carried up, will be exchanged with 7th. S.R.

6. Completion of relief will be sent by Code to Bn. Hqrs.

7. Sections will go into line at strength of 1 N.C.O. and 6 men.
   Platoon Hqrs. 1 Sgt.; 1 runner, 1 batmen.
   Coy. Hqrs.   2 scouts, 3 signallers, 2 runners, 4 S.Bs., 1 Gas
                  N.C.O. 1 batman, 2 sanitary.
   C.S. Majors of "B" and "D" Coys.

Personnel detailed to remain out of line and personnel in excess of above will proceed to RISPIN Camp (x 19 C 90 . 80.) on 2nd. June, arriving there before 1800.

Major E. Watson, M.C., will be in charge of these details, and he will send an officer to report to the Commandant there by 1000 for instructions as to accomodation.

[signature]

Capt. & Adjt.,
1/7th. Bn. H.L.I.

Copy No. 1. O.C. "A" Coy.
       2.   "B"
       3.   "C"
       4.   "D"
       5.   "H.Qs"
       6. T.O.
       7. Q.M.
       8. Major Watson
       9. W. Diary.
      10. do.
      11. Office.

SECRET.   Copy No.

   1/7th. (Blythswood) Battalion   The Highland Light Infantry.
     B A T T A L I O N   O R D E R S.
    By Lieut. Col. E. S. Gibbons, D.S.O., Commanding.   1/6/18.

   Battalion will parade at 1315 to-morrow, the 2nd. June and proceed to trenches.   Motor lorries will be provided to convey Battalion to a point on the road about 1000 yards W. of A 11 a 9. 9.   Lorries will be parked on the main road by FRASER CAMP.   Embussing will be carried out according to instructions recently circulated to Coy. Commanders.

   2 tins biscuits (50 lbs.) and 56 tins preserved meat are held at the following points :
       SPUR : B 14 a 5 6.   BORDER : B 13 a 4 9.
       TAPE : A 12 d 9 1.   FARBUS : B 7 d 7 7.
The above rations will be carefully checked and taken over by Coy. occupying the posts.   These rations will be shown on monthly reserve ration return.

   Transport will be brigaded at BERTHONVAL FARM, F 4 d 3 7. Q.Ms. party as detailed will be located at this place.   Move to be completed by 1400.

   All Officers' valises, Coy. Stores, etc. not required for trenches will be stacked at Q.M. Stores by 0830.

   Details for RISPIN CAMP will parade at 1430 under 2/Lieut. PULLAR. 2/Lieut. WYLIE will report to Commandant, RISPIN CAMP, at 1000 for accomodation for details.

   All huts and camp area must be left scrupulously clean on departure of Battalion.

                                                   Captain & Adjutant,
                                                    1/7th. Bn. H.L.I.

Copy No. 1.   O.C. "A" Coy.
      2.   "B"
      3.   "C"
      4.   "D"
      5.   "H.Qs"
      6.   T.O.
      7.   Q.M.
      8.   Major Watson.
  9, 10, and 11. W.D. and Office.

War Diary

SECRET.

WARNING ORDERS.

1. The Battalion will relieve the 4th Royal Scots in forward Subsection of the Left Divisional Sector, on Saturday, 29th June, 1918. Coys will relieve their respective Coys. of 4th Royal Scots.

2. Advance parties as under will go into the line on 28th June, parading at Battalion Headquarters, OTTAWA CAMP, at a time to be notified later.
    Intelligence Officer and Observers detailed.
    Signalling Officer and Signallers detailed.
    One Officer per Coy. One N.C.O. and one man per Platoon.
    Lewis Gun No. 1's.

27/6/18.

SECRET.

1/7th. (Blythswood) Battalion The Highland Light Infantry.

BATTALION ORDERS.

By Major E. Watson, M.C., Commanding.

7/6/18

The Battalion will relieve the 5th. Bn. H.L.I. in the forward area tomorrow, the 8th. instant, as detailed below :-
"A" Coy. will relieve "A" Coy. 5th. H.L.I. who will take over area, at present occupied by "B" Coy.
"B" Coy. will relieve "B" Coy. 5th. H.L.I. who will take over from "D" Coy.
"C" Coy. will relieve "D" Coy. 5th. H.L.I. who will take over from "C" Coy.
"D" Coy. will relieve "C" Coy. 5th. H.L.I. who will take over from "A" Coy.

ROUTES. "A" Coy. 7th. H.L.I. will commence moving at 1100, and proceed via TIRED ALLEY. Guides from 5th. H.L.I. will be at junction of TIRED ALLEY and BROWN LINE.
The platoon of "B" Coy. in SPUR POST will move at 0900 via TIRED ALLEY. Guide from 5th. H.L.I. will be at junction of Tired ALLEY and BROWN LINE. The Platoons in BURDEN, FARBUS and TAPE POSTS will move at 2100.
"C" Coy. will move out of posts in VANCOUVER ROAD at 0500 and will occupy POST LINE between WILLERVAL ROAD and ROWANT till 2000 when they will move up to new position via TIRED ALLEY. Guides of 5th. H.L.I. will be at junction of TIRED ALLEY and YUKON.
"D" Coy. will move at 1300 via BROWN LINE, BEEHIVE, and POST LINE. Guides from 5th. H.L.I. will be at junction of POST LINE and BEEHIVE.
Headquarters will move at 1500 via MERSEY ALLEY, BROWN LINE, TIRED ALLEY. Guide from 5th. H.L.I. will be at junction of TIRED ALLEY and POST LINE.

Guides will be found by Coys. for 5th. H.L.I. at following times and places :-
By "B" Coy. for "A" Coy. 5th. H.L.I. at junction of BROWN LINE and TIRED ALLEY at 1900 and 2100.
By "D" Coy. for "B" Coy. 5th. H.L.I. at junction of BROWN LINE and BEEHIVE at 1930 and 2130.
By "A" for "D" Coy. 5th. H.L.I. at junction of MERSEY ALLEY and BROWN LINE at 2030.
By "H.Qrs." for "H.Qs" 5th. H.L.I. at junction of MERSEY C.T. on top of VIMY RIDGE at 1600.

Movements by day will be by sections at not less than 100 yards distance, and not more than two platoons are to be on the move at the same time.
Advance parties will proceed as already detailed, and in addition Bn. Signallers will take over at 0800.
Lewis Guns will be carried up. Lewis Gun magazines camp kettles and periscopes will be taken over and handed over, also all trench and area stores.
Receipts for all above will be obtained. A limber will collect Bn. Hqr. stores at 2100, and "A" Coy. stores at junction of WILLERVAL ROAD and Railway Embankment.
"B" Coy. stores and Medical Officer's panniers will go by trolley from FARBUS junction and LONGWOOD respectively.
Coys. will report completion of relief to Bn. Hqrs. by code word "FOX".

X. Strachan
Lieut. A/Adjt.
1/7th. Bn. H.L.I.

7/6/18.

SECRET.   COPY NO. 9

1/7th. (Blythswood) Battalion   The Highland Light Infantry.

BATTALION ORDERS.

By Major E. Watson, M.C., Commanding.   13/6/18.

---

1. 7th. H.L.I. will be relieved in YUKON AREA by 5th. H.L.I. on 14th. June 1918.
   On relief 7th. H.L.I. will man positions in FARBUS AREA presently occupied by 5th. H.L.I.

2. Companies will take over as under :

5th. H.L.I.		7th. H.L.I.		5th. H.L.I.
A. Coy.	relieves	A. Coy.	which occupies area of	A. Coy.
B. Coy.	do.	B. Coy.	do.	B. Coy.
C. Coy.	do.	C. Coy.	do.	C. Coy.
D. Coy.	do.	D. Coy.	do.	D. Coy.

3. MOVE. 5th. H.L.I.

COY.	ROUTE.	TIME.	7TH. GUIDES AT	TIME.
A	TIRED ALLEY	0800	Junc. BROWN LINE & TIRED ALLEY.	0800.
B.	TIRED ALLEY.	1000	Junc. BROWN LINE & TIRED ALLEY.	1000.
C.	(BROWN LINE (MERSEY TRENCH	1200	Junc. BROWN LINE & MERSEY.	1200.
D.	2 Platoons TIRED ALLEY	1400	Junc. BROWN LINE & TIRED ALLEY	1400

   Above platoons for DURHAM and SUBURB POSTS.

   | D. | 2 Platoons BROWN LINE, BEEHIVE TRENCH, POST LINE. | 1400 | Junc. BROWN LINE & BEEHIVE TRENCH | 1400 |

   Above platoons for BARNSLEY and FOVANT POSTS.

   | H.QRS. | MERSEY, BEEHIVE, TIRED ALLEY and POST LINE. | 1500 | Junc. BROWN LINE & TIRED ALLEY. | 1500. |

   MOVE. 7th. H.L.I.
   Coys. on being relieved will move to their new areas by same routes taken by Coys. 5th. H.L.I. relieving them.

4. NEW AREA. DISPOSITION IN :
   A. COY. POSTS SPUR, FARBUS, BORDER 1 Platoon in each.
            TAPE, Coy. Hqs. and 1 platoon less 1 Section.
            No. 5 LIAISON POST, 1 Section (Riflemen).
            5th. H.L.I. guides will be at SPUR POST at 2100 to guide platoons to FARBUS, BORDER and TAPE POSTS.
   B. COY. BROWN LINE (right) 2 platoons.
            Coy. Hqrs. and 2 Platoons, less 1 section, behind RAILWAY EMBANKMENT.
            No. 4 LIAISON POST, 1 Section (Lewis Gun).
   C. COY. BROWN LINE (left) 2 platoons.
            Coy. Hqrs. and 2 platoons behind RAILWAY EMBANKMENT.
   D. COY. In reserve behind RAILWAY EMBANKMENT : if new "BLOB" posts are not ready at foot of VIMY RIDGE.
   BN. HQRS. At THELUS CAVE.

   Relief will be carried out as far as possible by daylight. Not more than two platoons of each Coy. should be on the move at same time. Movement will be by sections at 100 yards distance.

   Coys. will wire "priority" their departure from present area to Bn. Hqrs. using code word "ROBIN", and on taking over positions in new areas to Bn. Hqrs. at THELUS using code word "WREN".

5. ADVANCE PARTIES from 5th. H.L.I.

                           (over)

Battalion Orders (2)

per Coy. leaving present (1 Officer, 5 N.C.Os.
areas at 0800 day of (including Coy. Gas N.C.O.
relief (2 Signallers. 1 Cook.

Bn. Hqrs. leaving present (R.S.M.
area at 0800 (1 N.C.O.
(2 Signallers.
(Runners for relay posts.
(Bn. Gas N.C.O.

Signal stations and relay posts will be taken over from 7th. H.L.I. at 1150.

Scouts and observers. 1 Officer
1 N.C.O. and 6 men.

O.Ps. will be taken over from 7th. H.L.I. at 0600 day of relief.

Lewis Guns. L.G. Officer) leaving present
Gun No. 1's.) area at 0800.

6. ADVANCE PARTIES FROM 7th. H.L.I. *leaving 0800*
Per Coy. 1 Officer, 1 N.C.O. and 2 O.Rs.
Signallers : as arranged by Signalling Officer.
Observers : to new O.Ps. as soon as relieved at old.
DAISY BDE. O.P. 7th. H.L.I. will relieve 5th. H.L.I. at 0600

7. GUARDS ETC. *will be relieved as under   7th will relieve 5th H.L.I.*
Bde. Hqrs. Gas Guard (1 N.C.O. and 6 men) at 1200.
S.O.S. Posts by Coys. immediately on arrival in new positions.
Water - police on tanks 312, 314, 316 and Bde. Hqrs. at 1800.

8. STORES.
Area stores will be handed over and receipts obtained.
Regimental stores as detailed to Coy. Commanders will be handed over and receipts obtained.
Care will be taken that everything handed over is in a thoroughly clean condition.

9. CARRYING PARTIES.
D. Coy. will supply nightly Carrying Parties as under for 5th. H.L.I.
1 Officer (1 N.C.O. and 15 O.Rs.
(1 N.C.O. and 15 O.Rs. WATER.
(1 N.C.O. and 15 O.Rs.

(1 N.C.O. and 9 O.Rs.
(1 N.C.O. and 9 O.Rs. RATIONS.

These parties to be at LONGWOOD DUMP at dusk each evening to meet Ration train. Parties will always be properly armed and equipped.

10. BAGGAGE, RATIONS, WATER.
After order will be issued later.

Lieut. A/Adjt.
1/7th. H.L.I.

Copy No. 1. O.C. "A" Coy.
2. "B"
3. "C"
4. "D"
5. "H.Qs"
6. T.O. and Q.M.
7. O.C. 5th. H.L.I.
8. C.O.
9. War Diary
10. War Diary.
11. Office.

SECRET.   Copy No. 9

1/7th. (Blythswood) Battalion. The Highland Light Infantry.
B A T T A L I O N   O R D E R S.
By Major E. Watson, M.C., Commanding.

Ref. Map MAROEUIL 1/20,000.   19-6-18

1. 157th. Infantry Brigade will be relieved by 155th. Infantry Brigade
   in the WILLERVAL SECTION on 20th. June 1918.

2. Relief will be carried out in daylight, and to be completed by 6 a.m.
   on 21st. June.
       7th. H.L.I. will be relieved by 5th. K.O.S.Bs. in the FARBUS AREA.
   A., B., C., and D Coys. will be relieved by the same Coys. of 5th.
   K.O.S.Bs.

3. All communications, Trench maps, defence schemes and notes on work
   in progress will be handed over.

4. Advance parties of 5th. K.O.S.Bs. will arrive on the 19th. June.
   Guides for all posts and Companies will be at Bn. Hqrs. at 2.45 p.m.
   to take Advance Parties to their respective areas.

5. Relieving Battalions will arrive by Motor lorries 20th. June.
   Debussing point will be on NEUVILLE ST. VAAST – LES TILLEULS ROAD,
   600 yards West of Monumental Cross.   5th. K.O.S.Bs. will commence
   to arrive at debussing point about 1200.
       7th. H.L.I. will provide a chain of piquets under 2/Lieut. W. WEIR
   (who will be stationed at debussing point) along the tracks from the
   NEUVILLE ST. VAAST – LES TILLEULS ROAD to the junction TIRED ALLEY –
   VIMY RIDGE LINE.   This chain will be in position by 0845 on 20th.
   June and will remain till all relieving troops of 155th. Brigade
   have passed up.
       5th. K.O.S.Bs. will be directed by TIRED ALLEY.
   In addition to chain of guides Companies will provide adequate number
   of guides as follows :
       H.Qs. and A. Coy. : At debussing point at 1145.
       B., C., and D., Coys. : At junction of TIRED ALLEY and Railway
                               Embankment at 1200.

6. On relief 7th. H.L.I. will on leaving communication trenches move
   in sections at not less than 100 yards distance to embussing point
   NEUVILLE ST. VAAST – LES TILLEULS ROAD.   The motor lorries which
   bring up the relieving Battalions will convey relieved Battalions to
   their new areas at ST. NICK.
       Embussing Officer : Lieut. D. B. LOCKHART, Bn. Hqrs.
   Special instructions re travelling in lorries issued sometime ago
   will be adhered to strictly.   The Battalion will occupy OTTAWA
   CAMP vacated by 5th. K.O.S.Bs.

7. Captain J. A. LYLE will take over and make all arrangements
   regarding accommodation of Coys. prior to their arrival at OTTAWA
   CAMP on 20th. June.
       An Advance Party composed as under will proceed to OTTAWA CAMP
   from the Battalion on 20th. June leaving Bn. Hqrs. at 0900 :
       1 Officer and 6 O.Rs. per Coy.
   Officers will report to Capt. LYLE for instruction re accommodation
   and will have guides at entrance to Camp to guide platoons to Coy.
   Huts on their arrival.   Details at RIPPIN CAMP will move to OTTAWA
   CAMP and be there by 1200 on 20th. June.

8. Companies will notify Bn. Hqrs. that they have handed over to 5th.
   K.O.S.Bs. by priority wire using code-word "MAVIS".

                                                    J. F. Strachan.
                                                    Lieut. A/Adjt.
                                                    1/7th. Bn. H.L.I.

Issued at 0330 on 19/6/18

                        (P.T.O. for issue of copies)

Copy No. 1.   O.C. "A" Coy.
        2.   "B"
        3.   "C"
        4.   "D"
        5.   "H.Q."
        6.   C.O. and 2.C.
        7.   Capt. LYLE and Details.
        8.   R.S.M.
        9.   Orderly Room.
       10.   Orderly Room.

SECRET.   Copy No.

7TH. BN. H.L.I.   ADMINISTRATIVE INSTRUCTIONS
             Issued with reference to Battalion Orders
                    of   19th June 1918.

RELIEF.

(1) 7th. H.L.I. will be relieved by 8th. K.O.S.B. and will proceed on
    relief to OTTAWA CAMP on 20th. June.
    Details at RIGHT CAMP will move to OTTAWA CAMP on 20th. June by
    1800.
    Under orders of D.T.O. transport will move from present area to
    new camp by 1400 on 20th. June.

(2) O.C. Details will arrange direct with T.O. for any transport
    required for move.
    H.Qs. and Coys. in FORWARD AREA. Transport will be provided at usual
    ration delivery points on night of 19th. June for all surplus Coy.
    stores, blankets etc. These stores will be stacked at these points
    by 10 p.m. 19th. June.

(3) Area and Trench Stores, Soyer Stoves, Food Containers, Petrol tins
    and all trench stores will be handed over and receipts taken.
    Pro-forma lists issued to Coys. will be used. Copies will be
    handed in to Orderly Room by 1200 on 21st. June.
    Lewis Gun magazines, periscopes (box), and telephones will be
    exchanged as arranged by L.G.O. and Signalling Officer and O.C. Coys.
    AREA STORES at OTTAWA CAMP will be carefully checked by Advance
    Officers, and duplicates of receipts handed in to Orderly Room by
    1800 on 21st. instant.

(4) BILLET IMPROVEMENT.
    Units of the 2nd Brigade will hand over to relieving Units
    their scheme of work for billet sanitation and minor improvements
    and a schedule of the work in progress. This will include the
    construction of ovens, anti-aircraft protection etc.

(5) 7th. H.L.I. will be Bn. on duty on 21st. June. The following
    guards and picquets will be taken over by the Bn. and will mount
    as shown :

No.	Duty.	Strength.	Location.	Time.
(1)	Bde. Hqrs. Guard.	1 N.C.O. and 6 men.	Bde. Hqrs.	1700.
(2)	Picquet.	1 N.C.O., 3 men.	F.15.a.0.7.	1800 – 2100.
(3)	Picquet.	1 Officer, 3 N.C.Os. and 10 men.	F.15.a.7.9.	1800 – 2100.
(4)	Picquet.	1 N.C.O., 3 men.	F.15.b.9.0.	2100 – 2400.
(5)	Picquet.	1 N.C.O., 3 men.	F.15.a.4.4.	0900 – 2100.
(6)	To be held in readiness if called on. Officer will report at Bde. Hqrs.	1 Platoon		1800 – 2100.
(7)	Divisional Canteen	1 Sgt.	OTTAWA CAMP	1715 – 2100.
(8)	Camp Construction party.	100 men exclusive of Officers and N.C.Os. Half picks and half shovels.	R.E. Dump. FRASER CAMP.	0800 – 1200. 1300 – 1700.

(6) DISCIPLINE.
    N.C.Os. and men are forbidden to leave the Divnl. Area.
    BEGUINES and other villages in the 1st. Divn. Area i.e. South of
    and East and West line through Cross Roads F.15.c.1.1.) are
    strictly out of bounds for all units of the Brigade.

ADMINISTRATIVE INSTRUCTIONS (CONTINUED)

(7) **BOUNDS.**
The Bounds for the Brigade are marked by 52nd. Divnl. Boards at following points :
F.15a.1.7.
E.14.a.8.7.
F.15.b.6.8.
F.15.a.6.0.
F.1.d.6.7.

No N.C.O. or man is allowed outside these points without a Pass signed by the Commanding Officer and bearing the Office Stamp.

Battalion bounds will be marked by Battalion Boards (which have been issued).

No man will leave the area of the three camps at ST. ELOI without a belt.

It must be impressed on all men that they must be properly dressed and tidily dressed when going out of camp area.

(8) **BATHS.**
Baths at VILLERS AU BOIS (40 men each half-hour) are allotted to this Battalion on 21st. June from 0800 to 1700. Details will be issued later.

J. Strachan
Lieut. A/Adjt.,
1/7th. H.L.I.

19/6/18.

AFTER ORDER.

Reference para. 5, The following duties will also be taken over :

No.	Duty	Strength.	Location	
(16)	Water Picquet	1 Man	F.2.a.26.	Drinking.
		1 Man	F.2.c.14.	"

Men detailed for duty will report at 0900 on 20th. to Bn. Hqrs. of Bn. which is to be relieved.

Divisional Chaff Cutting Depot. To be furnished by Battalion on duty each day.

No.	Duty.	Strength.	Location.	Time.
(17)	Chaff Cutting.	1st. Shift 2 Sections.	Blackpool Sdg.	0730-1130.
		2nd. Shift 2 Sections.	A.7.d.4.2.	1400-1800.

Men detailed will report to N.C.O. a/c Divisional Chaff cutting Depot five minutes before their shift is due to start.

WATER PICQUETS.
(a) Chloride of Lime is required for all water tanks and is provided by the R.Q.O. of the unit finding the water picquet.
(b) The duties of water picquets are detailed in 52nd. Divnl. Circular Administrative Instructions No. 7 dated 24/6/18.
Orders in writing will be handed over by all picquets being relieved.

J. Strachan
Lt. A/Adjt
1/7th H.L.I.

War Diary. Volume III

July 1st to 31st 1918.

WAR DIARY
or
INTELLIGENCE SUMMARY

Army Form C. 2118.

1/7th H.L.I.

Volume III
1st to 31st July 1918.

Place	Date	Hour	Summary of Events and Information	Remarks and references to Appendices
VIMY	1/7/18		Day normal. 2 Sgt. 10 O.R. sick.	
do	2/7/18		At 1.10 a.m. four bombs landed in a "B" bay just (Tonk: "A" Coy.) Waiting sounds just occurring found in QUEBEC TRENCH (T.16.central) wounding 1 German officer and 1 O.R. in the next bay. Immediately the results of this bombing were made known an efforts of this coy. on the right (C coy) who this wounded and shelled enemy O.L. was seen by an officer of this coy. on the right (C coy) who this wounded and shelled enemy O.L. was The remainder of the enemy patrol estimated at 20 totals retiring across N/o Man's land were engaged by one of our patrols as follows:— 2 Platoon under 2/Lt. (?) McCadwell left off a position at T.II.a.61 at 12.30 a.m. and Cpl. Watson with 3 Scouts went forward from that to reconnoitre enemy post at T.II.a.85.30 Altho' owing through 100 yds they heard bombs behind them and returned to see if anything was all right. On its way back they encountered 2 Germans whom they instantly fired into and captured (wounded) the main party under 2/Lt. A. Pyle engaged the enemy patrol killing 8, wounding 5 (estimated) who escaped. Further information was supplied by wounded prisoner — enemy have consisted of 1 officer, 8 O.R. Killed; 3 O.R. wounded. Total enemy casualties — 1 officer, 8 O.R. Killed; 3 O.R. wounded. 2 unwounded & 2 wounded prisoners. Our casualties — 1 N.C.O. 4 O.R. wounded. Day quiet — artillery normal. At 10.45 hrs. patrol of 1 officer (A/C. R. E. P. Muir) with 1 section + L.G. team T.II.C.00 +43 to search ground in vicinity of T.II.a.6.1 to see if any German dead were lying there. On reaching T.II.a.50. they were challenged and bombs thrown at them. Shots were exchanged and enemy were found to be occupying both sides of the road. Patrol gradually withdrew to our lines.	Capt. Todd.

WAR DIARY or INTELLIGENCE SUMMARY

Army Form C. 2118.

1/7th H.L.I. Volume III 1st to 31st July 1918.

Place	Date	Hour	Summary of Events and Information	Remarks and references to Appendices
VIMY	2/7/18 (cont.)		At 11 p.m. patrol of 1 Offr. + 1 section left T.17.a.9.3 and T.17.c.6.0. and proceeded to T.17.b.5.6. and T.17.c.6.0. No enemy were seen. Patrol returned 2.15 am on 3/7/18. From hosp. Nil. To hosp. 4 O.R. Wounded. JDD	
do.	3/7/18		Enemy artillery more active on our forward area. Otherwise a quiet day. Patrols. (i) 1 Officer (2/Lt A.G. Walker) + 1 section with scouts + L.G. left T.17.b.9.3 at 10.45 p.m. and proceeded to T.18.a.2.8. Where they reconnoitred enemy wire. Patrol returned at 1 am. (2) Defensive patrol 1 N.C.O., 2 B.N. scouts + ½ L.G. section went out and took up a position at T.11.c.0.1. at 11 p.m. - withdrawing at 2 am. From hosp. 3 O.R. sick. 19 O.R. draft. To hosp. 2 O.R. sick 1 O.R. wounded. JDD	
do.	4/7/18		A quiet day. 10 am to 10.30 am all ranks wore S.B.R. for practise. Patrols. Defensive patrol of 1 N.C.O., 2 B.N. scouts + ½ L.G. section took up position at T.17.C. central at 11 p.m. returning at 2 am with nothing to report. From hosp. nil. To hosp. 3 O.R. sick JDD	
do.	5/7/18		Usual quiet day. One Reinforcements from 10 am to 10.30 am JDD From hosp. 6 O.R. sick. To hosp. 3 O.R. sick JDD	
do.	6/7/18		No enemy activity. One Reinforcements from from 10 am to 10.30 am. At 3.20 p.m. 2 aircraft (Patrol) belonging to the 46th I.D. surrendered to our advanced post in TOPER. Patrols:- (1) Defensive patrol of 1 Officer ½ L.G. section and 2 B.N. scouts left T.10.d.4.1 at 11 p.m. + took up position at T.10.d.4.7 - returning at 2 am during am no enemy. (2) Defensive patrol of 1 Sergt. ½ L.G. section and 2 B.N. scouts left T.17.a.3.8 at 11 p.m. and took up position at T.11.d.0.0. returning at 2 am. with nothing to report. To hosp. 2 O.R. sick JDD	

Army Form C. 2118.

WAR DIARY
or
INTELLIGENCE SUMMARY.
(Erase heading not required.)

1/7th H.L.I.

Volume III

1st to 31st July 1918.

Place	Date	Hour	Summary of Events and Information	Remarks and references to Appendices
VIMY	7/7/18		Enemy artillery active in the morning at midday and at night - CANADA TRENCH and the vicinity of MONT FORET QUARRIES shelled at these times with 5.9's and 4.2's. Enemy aeroplane was brought down near LA CHAUDIERE. Patrols (1) 2/Lt W.H. McCallum with 1 section & 2 N. Scouts and 1 L.G. left T.7.c.6.0. at 2310 and had just reached our wire when heavy enemy shelling commenced. Patrol pushed forward 200x. and took up position T.17.d.2.4. and returned at 0215 with nothing further to report. (2) On patrol of 1 Sgt. & 1 L.G. section was leaving T.11.C.0.1. enemy opened T.M. fire on QUARRIES ROAD. Patrol took up a position at T.11.C. central, sighted no enemy and returned at 0200. Whole 1 O.R. sick. 10 O.R. wounded. S/S.	
do.	8/7/18		Very quiet day. Enemy aircraft more active than usual, especially from 1800-1900. Patrols: 2/Lt. McCormack with 1 L.G. section left T.16 & 2.1. at 2300. Took up position at T.11.d.0.0. and returned at 0250 having seen no enemy. Enemy Snipers 8 O.R. sick 2 O.R. with 10%/wounded. S/S	
do.	9/7/18		Great activity among our planes. About 11 a.m. a hostile plane, while chasing one of ours was attacked by another turned towards enemy lines but was hit by m.g. fire from our aircraft, plane and crashed near FARBUS. Several aeroplane patrols at night. Enemy Snipers 2 O.R. sick. Whole 1 O.R. sick. Lt. H.P. Toppan to 3rd Div. L.T.M.B's. Strength.	
do.	10/7/18		Uneventful & quiet day. Enemy Snipers 2 O.R. sick - draft 20 O.R. 2 Sgts. J. Brodie (2/Lt. Cheesbourne) 2 O.R. out. 1 O.R. wounded. S/S	

Capt. A.O. Byars a/Lt. Col.
Comdg. 1/7 Glasgow (L/t. Highland Light Infantry)

Army Form C. 2118.

WAR DIARY
or
INTELLIGENCE SUMMARY.
(Erase heading not required.)

1/7th A.H.L.I.   Volume III   1st to 31st July 1918.

Place	Date	Hour	Summary of Events and Information	Remarks and references to Appendices
VIMY	11/7/18		Batn. was relieved in front line sector by 6th A.H.L.I. and moved into reserve, occupying BROWN LINE from GRAND TRUNK to CYRIL TRENCH. Relief complete by 1400. From hosp. 2 O.R. sick. To hosp. 2 O.R. sick. 1 O.R. wounded. G.S.	
do.	12/7/18		Day quiet. Enemy bombarded yards the sector. General Hunter Weston. 2400 yards of our artillery discharge in our front attempt. Batn. subbed 400 men unsatisfactorily. From hosp. nil. To hosp. 2 O.R. sick. Officers (Capt. H. E. Jenkins) taken on effective strength	
do.	13/7/18		Enemy artillery fired about 200 H.E.'s mostly "duds" – otherwise quiet. Wire carried on. To hosp. 2 O.R. sick. G.S.	
do.	14/7/18		Day quiet. About 200 gas shells fell in front of BROWN LINE near LA CHAUDIERE about 2300 — no effect felt by our men. From hosp. 2 O.R. sick. Batn. 10 O.R. To hosp. 1 O.R. sick G.S.	
do.	15/7/18		Dispositions altered owing to change on Divisional + Bde frontiers. Boundaries two right coys were relieved by 1/8 S.R. two divisions there three coys in BROWN LINE from S.P.A.4.8 to CYRIL TRENCH. and one coy in LA CHAUDIERE area — change complete by 2000. From hosp. 1 O.R. sick. To hosp. 3 O.R. sick. G.S.	
do.	16/7/18		Day spent drying alts. very wet night. Were kept in CHAUDIERE. SPUR sighted Havana Trench & MOKO yard - Patrolled attention given to three new tiers at night. From hosp. 1 O.R. sick. From Egypt 1 O.R. To hosp. nil.	

WAR DIARY

Army Form C. 2118.

Volume VII
1st to 31st July 1918

1/4th A.L.I.

Place	Date	Hour	Summary of Events and Information	Remarks and references to Appendices
ST. ELOY	17/7/18		Bn relieved. Bath returned by H.Q's and engaged in trials to ST ELOY. Two days and N.C.Os were camped in SUBURBAN CAMP and this was in LEPENDU CAMP. Shelling forced the batln from reception camp. Rations complete at 1630. Batn complete at 2000. Gnrs hosp. 31 ords. 1 wounded. Draft 9 to hosp. 1. O.R. Sick. ½t	
do.	18/7/18		Day spent in cleaning up. All ops. at 16 later. Gnrs hosp. 2 ors. sick To hosp. 4. O.R. sick. ½t	
do.	19/7/18		[illegible] Physical drill. [illegible] strength [illegible] gns hospn was reinforced. Batn moved to DURHAM & LANCASTER CAMPS at 0900. One new draft arrived not heavy. 1099 (1/Lt J [illegible]) 1 or & 105 from draft. 2 offrs (2/Lt Lt J Kilman) 42 O.R. sick [illegible] 2 ors. ½t	
AUCHEL	20/7/18		Bath paraded 0800 and marched to ST. ELOY station entrained there at 1000. detrained at CALONNE RICOUART and marched to billets in AUCHEL. To hosp. 1 O.R. sick. ½t	
do.	21/7/18		Day spent in settling down. Church parade 1100. To hosp. 1 offr (Capt. [illegible]) & 2 or sick	
do.	22/7/18		0830 - 1200 Physical Drill, close order drill. Arry an BOIS DES DAMES DANZE 1400 - 1500 Lectures. N.C.Os from hosp. N.g. 2/Lt Col. Vallance 1 o.r. L.I.M.B. taken on strength. to hosp. 3 o.r. sick - 2 offrs 2/Lt N.G. Wilson & 2/Lt R.J. Mitchell to RAF. Strength of strength. ½t	

WAR DIARY / INTELLIGENCE SUMMARY

Army Form C. 2118.

Volume III
1st to 31st July 1918

Place	Date	Hour	Summary of Events and Information	Remarks and references to Appendices
AUCHEL	23/7/18		Training same as previous day. Strict church parade from 1000-1700. Major Graham M.C. 1400-1500 lecture to all N.C.O.s & 2/Lts. Gave lecture 2b O.R. sick. 6 O.R. wounded. Draft to officers 2/Lt Campbell, Capton Crawford & Erickson) and 29 O.R.	
do	24/7/18		From 12 noon on 23rd instant the Division was in G.H.Q. Reserve. 187 O.R. ready & moving two hours in 6 hours notice. Training as previous day. From hosp 1 officer and 6 O.R. Draft 48 O.R. To hosp 3 O.R. sick. 6 O.R.	
do	25/7/18		Training as previous day. To hosp. 4 O.R. sick.	
do	26/7/18		Coy elementary tactical schemes - artillery & attack formations practised - From hosp 6 O.R. sick. From R.M.S. Sept 2 O.R. Drummer tried Sept 7 O.R & 1 O.R. To hosp 3 O.R. sick.	
do	27/7/18		Elementary summaries tactical training. Concert in AUCHEL CINEMA in the evening. To hosp. 2 O.R. sick.	
do	28/7/18		Church parade 1000. Remainder summaries about cleaning equipment to prepare. From hosp. 5 O.R. sick. To hosp. 3 O.R. sick.	
do	29/7/18		0830 Battn marched by coys to training area in C.23 (R.& Maps sheet 44 B 1/40,000) arriving at Station (School numbers were carried out till 1200. The shot above for N.C.O.s and Lewis gunners was wonderful, invisible and excellent. Demonstration under the Midnight from 1400-1500 From hosp. 4 O.R.	
do	30/7/18		To hosp. 9 O.R. sick. Bn. marched from AUCHEL via CAMBLAIN-CHATELAIN & HOUDAIN & BARLIN to camp in BOIS D'OHLAIN near BARLIN. To hosp. 4 O.R.	

WAR DIARY
or
INTELLIGENCE SUMMARY.

(Erase heading not required.)

Army Form C. 2118.

Place	Date	Hour	Summary of Events and Information	Remarks and references to Appendices
	30/7/18		Bn. marched via VERDREL, VILLERS AU BOIS, MONT ST ELOY, ANZIN ST AUBIN, to MADAGASCAR AREA. Battn. arrived in MAROEUIL camp near BOCKINGHAM at about 1900 – march was chiefly at ease. Filtration began. Bn. going into Trenches following day – Ammunition went round out night to ECOIVRES. In Trenches 10 R. Gasualties. nil	

	O	OR	Total			O	OR	Total
From Hosp. Sick. usual	1	114	115	L. Regt. Sick usual		3	82	85
Draft	4	139	143	To Base		10	10
Rejoined		5	5	To 30th Divn		3	3
Return on ∝		1		L. T. R. A. T.	1		1
& Hospital stampers	4	5	5		2		2
Total	9	267	276	Total	6	95	101

SECRET.   COPY NO. 10

1/7th (Blythswood) Battalion – The Highland Light Infantry.

B A T T A L I O N   O R D E R S.
By Lieut-Colonel E.S. Gibbons, D.S.O., Commanding.
10th July, 1918.

———————

1. The 6th H.L.I. will relieve the 7th H.L.I., in the Right
   Sub Section on the 11th inst.,

2. Companies will take over as under:-
       6th H.L.I.   7th H.L.I.
       A. Coy.....relieves........A. Coy.
       B. Coy.....   do   ......C. Coy.
       D. Coy.....   do   ......B. Coy.
       C. Coy.....   do   ......D. Coy.

   Companies of the 7th H.L.I. will take over corresponding
   areas in the Support line from 6th H.L.I. by whom they are
   relieved.

3. MOVE.
   Each Coy. will send one Section per Platoon in Black
   Line to the new area at 3a.m. Guides for these Sections and
   for the Companies, when relieved (one guide per platoon) will
   be furnished by 6th H.L.I. at the following points:-
   For A. Coy.7.H.L.I, - Junction of GRAND TRUNK & TOAST.
   For B. Coy. do...... Junction of JAMES & GERTIE.
   For C. Coy. do...... Junction of CANADA & PEGGIE.
   For D. Coy. do...... Junction of CANADA & PEGGIE.
   For Hdqrs.   do...... At Cross Roads - T. & C.T.4.
   The guides for the above Sections will be at places at 0600.
   Companies of 7th H.L.I. will also furnish guides at the above
   points for 6th H.L.I. at 0730. (one per platoon and one for HQ)

4. STORES.
   All trench and area stores, log books, etc., will be handed
   over. Lewis Gun Magazines will be handed over except 10
   magazines per gun, which will be carried. The one day's
   rations (reserve) at present held by Companies, will be handed
   over and similar rations held by 6th H.L.I. will be taken over.
   Any necessary alterations regarding the numbers of these rations
   will be adjusted by Companies.
   Receipts for Stores handed over and taken over will be
   rendered to this Office by 2000 on the 11th July, 1918.

5. RELIEF.
   Any movement of relief which may take place over the open
   will be by Sections at not less than 100yds. distance. Relief
   to be completed by 9p.m. Completion of relief will be wired
   Battalion Headquarters by Code word "SALLY".

                                 J.A. Strachan.
                                 LIEUT. & A/ADJT.
                                 1/7th Bn. H.L.I.

Copy No. 1   O.C. A. COY.
          2   B. Coy.
          3   C. Coy.
          4   D. Coy.
          5   Hdqrs.,
          6   T.O.,
          7   Q.M.,
          8   S.O.,
          9   War Diary.
         10   do
         11   Office.

AFTER ORDER.
   All L.G. Magazine tin boxes, canvas carriers and web
pouches will be carried to the new area; only loaded magazines will
be handed over.

SECRET.   COPY NO. 10

1/7th (Blythswood) Battalion - The Highland Light Infantry.

BATTALION ORDER.
By Major H. Watson, M.C., Commanding.

14th July, 1918.

TRENCH MAP - LA TARGETTE 1/20,000.
(TRENCH SHEET 44A - (25c) S.W. 1/20,000.

1. The 52nd Divisional Inter Brigade Boundary, will be altered on 15th July, 1918, to the following co-ordinates.
T.10 c.0.0. thence junction VESTA FILLET & TRUDIE GERARD trenches, thence junction of JULIA J and GEORGIE trenches about T.14d.0.0, thence junction PERRIE C.T. & RAILWAY EMBANKMENT, about T.19 b.8.3, thence along N. side GEORGIE TR. to S.14 d.4.8. thence S.24 c.0.7.

2. Consequent on above, the following moves will take place, on 15th July, and night of 15/16 July. Relief to be completed by 6 a.m. 16th July, 1918.

    (a) 4th R.S. will take over line held by 6th H.L.I. who will proceed to HANSON CAMP, NEUVILLE ST. VAAST.

    (b) 7th S.R. will take over portion of BROWN LINE presently held by A. & C. Coys. 7th H.L.I. as far as S.14 d.4.8.

    (c) A. & C. Coys. 7th H.L.I. will "side step" to the North along BROWN LINE. "D" Coy. closing up to the left. "B" Coy. will continue to hold CHAUDIERE AREA. Company boundaries as pointed out to O.C. Companies.

    (d) 8th H.L.I. will not move.
    A. & C. Companies will move on relief by 7th S.R. O.C. A.Coy will wire Battn. Hdqrs. when commencing to move, using code word "START".
    In the event of an alarm or enemy attack during the relief troops will halt and man nearest trenches of tactical importance and report disposition immediately to Bn. Hdqrs.

3. All Trench Stores with the undernoted exceptions, taken over from 6th H.L.I. on 11/7/18 will be handed over to 7th S.R.Coys. by O.C. A. & C. Coys., Receipts being obtained for same.
    Exceptions above mentioned.- Soyer Stoves; Food Containers; Petrol Tins; Lewis Gun Drums etc., which will be brought to new area. Ration Dumps at VIMY (S.24 d.6.4.) and CULVERT (T.10 c.2.2.) will also be handed over and receipts obtained. The usual pro-forma will be used for Trench Stores handed over, and will be sent to Battn. Headquarters by 1800 on 15/7/18.

4. O.C. "A" & "C" Coys. will also hand over to relieving Coys. 7th S.R. any special maps and plans regarding Coy. area taken over from 6th H.L.I., also all information regarding work in hand and work projected.

5. Completion of ~~relief~~ occupation of new area will be wired to Battn. Hdqrs. using Code word "JUSTSO"

J. Strachan.
LIEUT. & A/ADJT.
1/7th Bn. H.L.I.,

ISSUED AT:- 2100
Copy 1 O.C. A.Coy.
     2   B.
     3   C.
     4   D.
     5   Hd.Qrs.
     6   T.M.
     7   O.C.
     8   C.O.
     9   War Diary.
    10   Office

SECRET.   COPY NO:- 12

1/7th (Blythswood)   Battalion - The Highland Light Infantry.
BATTALION   ORDER.
By Major E. Watson, M. C., Commanding.
15th July, 1918.
-:-:-:-:-:-:-:-:-:-:-:-:-:-:-:-:-:-

1. The 155th Infantry Brigade will relieve the 157th Infantry Brigade on 17th and night of 17/18th July, 1918.

2. The 4th K.O.S.B. will relieve the 7th H.L.I. in the BROWN LINE. The 7th H.L.I., will withdraw via BLIGHTY Trench on relief. While on the enemy side of the VIMY RIDGE, a distance of at least 200 yards will be maintained between Platoons.
   Particular care must be taken to prevent any movement being observed by the enemy.

3. Whilst in Divisional Reserve the 7th H.L.I., will Occupy LE PENDE and SUBURBAN Camps (2 Coys. in each).

4. Lieut. A.G. Clark, will on 16th July, 1918, see Camps to be occupied and make all arrangements <u>re</u> accommodation of Coys. and arrange to have guides at the entrance to Camp on MONT ST. ELOI - ACQ road on 17th July, 1918.

5. O.C. Coys. will prepare and hand over all Defence Schemes, special maps,&details of work in hand and work projected in writing for the new Coy. areas, to the incoming Unit.

6. In the event of an alarm or attack during the relief, troops will halt and man the nearest defences of tactical importance reporting their position to nearest Battn. Headquarters.

7. Completion of relief by 4th K.O.S.B. will be wired to present Battn. Headquarters, using Code word "POPOFF"

8. Administrative Instructions are attached.

9. Programme of training /whilst in Divl. Reserve will be issued later.

10. ACKNOWLEDGE.

ISSUED AT:- 2230.

J. Strachan.

LIEUT. & A/ADJT.
1/7th Bn. H.L.I.,

Copy No 1.   O.C. A. Coy.
        2.   B.
        3.   C.
        4.   D.
        5.   Hdqrs.
        6.   T.O.
        7.   Q.M.
        8.   Lt. Clark.
        9.   C.O.
       10.   R.S.M.
       11.   War Diary.
       12.   do.
       13.   Office.

ADMINISTRATIVE INSTRUCTIONS
issued with BATTALION ORDERS of 15/7/18.
-:-:-:-:-:-:-:-:-:-:-:-:-:-:-

REFERENCE SHEET 51C. N.E.

1. Relief of Duties.-
Water Point Duties furnished by this Battalion in VIMY - CHAURIERE area will be handed over to relieving Unit.

2. TRANSPORT.
Transport Lines and permanent Q.M. Stores will remain as at present in ROSS CAMP.

3. SUPPLIES.
Rations for 18th July will be drawn as at present from LEADLEY SIDING; rations for the consumption from 19th July, will be drawn from BLACKPOOL SIDING.

4. WATER.
Water is laid on in LE PENDE & SUBURBAN CAMPS. The Regtl. Sergeant Major will arrange for police for all taps and tanks to prevent waste.

5. LORRIES.
The motor lorries which bring up Coys. of relieving Unit will be available to convey Battalion to new Camp.
Brigade Embussing Officers :- Lieut. Stewart J.M. and
Lieut., Nicholson.

6. TRENCH & AREA STORES.
Soyer Stoves; food Containers; petrol tins and all trench Stores will be handed over and receipts obtained. Instructions regarding L.G. Drums etc., will be communicated on completion of negotiations with 4th K.O.S.B. by Lewis Gun Officer.
Area store Lists as per pro-forma, and instructions laid down carefully complied with, will be sent to Battn. Headquarters by 1000 on 19th July, 1918.

7. BILLET IMPROVEMENTS.
Lieut. A.G. Clark will receive from Unit presently occupying LE PENDE & SUBURBAN CAMPS their scheme of work for billet sanitation and minor improvements and a schedule of the work in progress. Lieut. Clark will also take over any area stores in the 2 Camps.
Copy of the receipt given will be handed into Battn. Orderly Room.

8. DUTIES.
Battalion on Duty 18th July............6th H.L.I.,
Next for Duty..........................7th H.L.I.,
Next for Duty..........................5th H.L.I.,
and subsequently in this order.
The following Guards and Picquets will be furnished by Battn. on duty:-

DUTY.	STRENGTH.	LOCATION.	TIME TO REPORT.
Bde. Hdqrs.Guard.	1 N.C.O. 6 men.	Bde. Hdqrs.)	1700.
Police.	1 Regtl. Police man at each point.	F.15.a.0.7.) F.14.a.7.5.) F.13.b.8.6.) F.13.a.2.7.) F.1.a.4.2.)	
Divl. Canteen.	1 Sergeant.	OTTAWA CAMP.	1715 - 2030.

The Battalion on Duty will detail one Company to report to Transport Lines at 0900 for improvement work, 1 Platoon being detailed to each Battalion, and 1 to Brigade Hdqrs. These Platoons will be from work under orders of Os.C. Units to whom they report. Work will be from 0900 - 1200.
Battalion on duty will also detail one Platoon to report to Area Commandant, ST. ELOI at 0800. This Platoon will take its meals in Divl. Cookery School.

CONTD/-

2.

DUTIES (Ctd).

DUTIES TO BE FURNISHED BY BATTALION.
(c) By 7th H.L.I.

DUTY.	STRENGTH.	LOCATION.	
Water Picquet.	1 man.	W.25.c.4.1.	Horses.
	1 man.	(W.30.d.8.1.	Horses.
		(E. 6.b.8.8.	Horses.
	1 man.	F.1.d.3.2.	Drinking.
	1 man.	(F.8.c.5.9.	Tank.
		(F.8.c.5.6.	Drinking.
	1 man.	(F.4.d.1.2.	Horses.
		(F.4.d.2.1.	Drinking.

Men detailed for water duty by R.S.M. for above, will report at Battn. Headquarters, at a time on 16th July to be notified later by the Regtl. Sergt. Major. Written instructions for the post they man will be given them.

Water Picquets.
(a) Chloride of lime is required for all water tanks and is provided by M.O. of Unit finding water picquet.

(b) The duties of the water Picquet will be read to them on parade Orders etc. in writing will be handed over by Picquets being relieved
Each Battalion will detail 10 men daily for Camp Improvement and Sanitation under Regtl. arrangements.
The Brigade Transport Officer will detail one Maltese Cart complete with team and driver to be attached to the Divl. Reception Camp during the period the Brigade is in Reserve.

9. BATHS.
Baths are allotted to 7th H.L.I. as under:-

ST. ELOI BATHS.
40 men each half hour.
18th July.   1100 - 1200...............80 men.
              1300 - 1700...............320 men.
                                        400 men.

VILLERS AU BOIS BATHS.
40 men each half hour.
18th July.   0800 - 1200...............320 men.
              1300 - 1700...............320 men.
                                        640 men.

The hours for Coy. Parades at Baths will be notified later.

10. AREAS.
Coy. areas in BROWN LINE will be handed over to 4th K.O.S.B. in a clean and sanitary state and receipts obtained.

11. DISCIPLINE.
N.C.Os. and men are forbidden to leave the Divl. area. ECOIVRES and other villages in the 51st Divln. Area (i.e. South of an EAST abd WEST line through Cross Roads F.14.b.10.6.) are strictly out of Bounds for all Units of the Brigade.

12. BOUNDS.
The Bounds for the Brigade are marked by 52nd Divl. Boards at the/-

CONTD/3

BOUNDS (Ctd).
The following points:-
F.15.a.1.7.
F.14.a.8.7.
F.13.b.8.6.
F.13.a.9.9.
F. 1.d.5.2.

No N.C.O. or man is allowed outside these points without a pass signed by the Commanding Officer and bearing the Orderly Room Stamp.
Battalion Bounds will be marked by Battalion Boards.
No man will leave the area of the three Camps at ST. ELOI without a belt.
It must be impressed on all men that they must be properly and tidely dressed when going out of Camp Area.
Steps will be taken to see that this is carried out.

J B Strachan

LIEUT. & A/ADJT.
1/7th Bn. H. L. I.,

Copy No. 10.

1/7th. (Blythswood) Battalion   The Highland Light Infantry.

WARNING ORDER.

Reference Maps LENS 11.   )
              HAZEBROUCK 5a) 1/100,000.

1. Whilst in the present area the Division is in G.H.Q. Reserve.

2. The 157 Brigade Group will be ready to move, by bus, or train, on six hours notice.

3. DRESS.
   1. Packs will only be carried in action when rations issued amount to more than can be carried in a haversack and mess tin. In the event of the Brigade being ordered to take part in an action and when no further rations than normally carried by a man are issued, packs would not be carried, but would be dumped under Brigade arrangements and haversacks carried.
   2. Packs if carried will contain:-
      Balmoral : Rations : Mess tin : Knife, fork, spoon : Razor : Soap : Towel : Spare socks : One spare shirt : cardigan : oil tin and flannellette : Waterproof sheet (attached outer flap of pack) : Haversack (empty). The latter only to be used for carrying bombs and additional S.A.A. when issued and then to be worn in the usual way.
         Careful attention must be paid to seeing that men do not fill up their packs with anything else thereby increasing the weight.
   3. Greatcoats will be carried over the arm and dumped at debussing point or detraining station. They will always be dumped before going into action.

4. TOOLS.
   On the order to move by bus or train being received each Company will at once draw from the Q.M. Stores 19 picks and 20 shovels.

5. Intelligence Officer will have two trained observers detailed ready to report to Brigade Headquarters immediately orders to move are received.
   They will take two days' rations with them.

6. As a nucleus will probably be left behind, O.C. Coys. will have their nucleus personnel told off forthwith in accordance with establishment issued to Companies on 23rd. June, 1918.

1 MOVE BY BUS.

1. Head of the Embussing Point is at X in CHAUCY LA TOUR. Notice boards have been placed at each end of the embussing point. All Officers will reconnoitre the road to embussing point both by day and by night, forthwith.

2. A Bus takes : 1 Officer and 25 Other Ranks.
   A Lorry takes : 1 Officer and 20 Other Ranks.

3. All Lewis Guns will be carried, and 24 magazines per gun in tin boxes.

4. At least one day's rations will be carried on the man.

5. TOOLS. From billets to embussing point the tools drawn from the Q.M. Stores will be carried on the man. There will be lorries provided for the purpose to take them from there.

SECRET.

AFTER ORDER.
By Major E. Watson M.C., Commanding
1/7th Bn, H.L.I.
15/7/18.

-:-:-:-:-:-

ADVANCE PARTY. of 4th K.O.S.B. will report tomorrow 16th July,
Guides. 1 guide from Hdqrs. will meet advance party at Bde. Hdqrs. at 1000. 1 guide per Coy. will meet the party at junction of BLIGHTY and BROWN LINE at 10-30.
Guides for 4th K.O.S.B. on day of relief - 17th, will be at same points at 1100 and 1130 respectively.

BAGGAGE. As much as possible will be sent over by returning Ration Limbers tomorrow, Tuesday night. O.C. Coys. will state by 9a.m. 17th what transport they will require to lift baggage on Wednesday night.

LIEUT. & A/ADJT.
1/7th Bn. H.L.I.

(2).

6. **TRANSPORT.**
Transport will move by road.

MOVE BY TRAIN.

1. The Brigade Group will be allotted two tactical trains and one omnibus train. Each tactical train holds 1750 - 2000 men. An omnibus train is designed to carry both transport and personnel.

2. The entraining station will be PERNES.
At least two officers per Coy. will reconnoitre the road to the station both by day and by night forthwith.

3. **LEWIS GUNS.**
Lewis Guns and Magazines will go in limbers.

4. **TOOLS**
Tools drawn from Q.M. Stores will be carried on the man to entraining station, and taken on the tactical trains.
A lorry will be provided if necessary at the detraining station to bring these forward until the tool limbers arrive by road.

5. **TRANSPORT.**
All transport, except what goes on omnibus train, will proceed by road.
Transport carried by omnibus train per Battalion is :

(1) <u>Table A.</u>

	O.Rs.	Horses
4 L. G. Limbers	8	8
3 Field Cookers	3	6
1 Water Cart	1	2
10 Chargers	10	10
6 Packs	6	6.

(2) <u>Table B.</u>

4 L. G. Limbers	8	8
2 Field Cookers	2	4
10 Chargers	10	10
6 packs	6	6.

An order to move will state whether the move will be according to Table A or Table B.

J. Strachan.

Lieut. & A/Adjt.,
1/7th. Bn. H.L.I.

Copy No. 1. O.C. A. Coy.
2. B.
3. C.
4. D.
5. H.Q.
6. T.O.
7. Q.M.
8. C.O.
9. R.S.M.
10. War Diary
11. do
12. Office.

SECRET. Copy No. 18

1/7TH. BN. HIGHLAND LIGHT INFANTRY.   MOVE ORDERS.

By Major E. Watson, M.C., Commanding.   29/7/18

Reference Map :   LENS 11, HAZEBROUCK 5a, 1/100,000

1. The XV11th. Corps will relieve the CANADIAN Corps in the ARRAS Sector.
Infantry relief will probably commence on night of 31st. July/1st. August, 1918.
52nd. Division will occupy the left Subsector of the Corps front, all three Brigades in the line.
To-morrow, the 30th. July, 1918, the 157th. Infantry Brigade Group will move by road to billets in BARLIN.

2. Battalion will parade in close column of Companies, H.Qs. A., B., C., and D. Coys., ready to move at 0800 to-morrow, the 30th. July, 1918, on RUE D'AIRE Parade ground, C.22.c. (Ref. Map Sheet 44 B.
ROUTE :- AUCHEL - CAMBLAIN CHATELAIN - HOUDAIN.
Distance between Units to be maintained as laid down in Battalion Order No. 355 dated 27/7/18.
Ten minutes halts will take place at 10 minutes to each clock hour, times to be strictly adhered to.
When and if necessary the usual precautions against hostile aircraft will be taken.

3. ADVANCE PARTY.   Lieut. R. E. R. Muir, and one N.C.O. each from A. C. and D. Coys. proceed to-day to BARLIN by Lorry. Leaving Brigade Headquarters at 1300.

4. TRANSPORT.   Transport will move with Battalion. Limbers will be loaded to-night and parked at Transport Lines. Guard will be detailed by R.S.M.   Lewis Guns will be carried by limber.
Officers baggage, mess boxes, and Company stores will be delivered at Q.M. Stores by 0700 to-morrow.   Field Cookers, immediately after breakfast, will be taken to Transport Lines.   Transport Officer will have transport ready to fall in in rear of the Battalion when Battalion pass Transport Lines.

5. ROUTINE.   Reveille :- 0500.
   Breakfast :- 0600.
   Sick parade :- 0630.

6. DRESS.
Full marching order, packs will be carried by men : balmorals will be worn, steel helmets carried on back of packs.

7. RATIONS.
Rations for to-morrow will be carried on the man, except meat portion of ration.

J. Strachan
Lieut. & A/Adjt.
29/7/18.   1/7th. Bn. H.L.I.

Copy No. 1.   O.C. A. Coy.
        2.   B.   Copy No. 6.   C.O.
        3.   C.   7.   Q.M.
        4.   D.   8.   T.O.
        5.   H.Qs.   9.   R.S.M.

War Diary Volume III
August 1st to 31st - 1915

Army Form C. 2118.

WAR DIARY
or
INTELLIGENCE SUMMARY.
(Erase heading not required.)

Volume III
1st to 31st August 1918.

1/4th K.L.R.

Place	Date	Hour	Summary of Events and Information	Remarks and references to Appendices
OPPY SECTION	1/8/18		The Bttn moved into the line. The Battalion relieved portions of the 10th Canadian Infantry Bn. and of the 135th & 156th Bgds. Batns. Personnel lice. TOMMY ASHEY in command of coy's 2 TIRED MILLEY deceasive with south. Relief complete about 12.00. The day was quiet except for a five minutes intense bombardment of the front line on our right by 105 and 77 mm guns at 10.45 am. Patrols 2/Lt B.H. Pallar with one rifle section and 1/2 R.G. section left BOH TRENCH at ARLEUX Rd. ascertained ARLEUX LOOP SOUTH at B.5.c.8.8. Patrol.	A
do.	2/8/18		R.D. pursued along the road & reconnoitred ARLEUX LOOP SOUTH at B.5.c.8.8. Patrol. No challenges met and after waiting a time withdrew reaching own line at 1.30 am. from bnd. 2 O.R. sick. To hosp. 2 O.R. sick.	
do.	3/8/18		Hostile artillery normal Preparations made for impending European attack. North and heavier shoots from hosp. 2 OR sick. To hosp. 9 OR sick Diagnosed - slight gas shelling with yuccares at night. Returned 1 OR enters the front during the night. from hosp. 3 OR sick. To hosp. 1 OR wounded 2 O.R. sick	
do	4/8/18		Marginal. Work on ? trenches being continued. Defensive R & D at night. from hosp. 6 O.R. sick. To hosp. 2 O.R. sick.	
do.	5/8/18		Normal. from hosp. 5 OR sick. To hosp. 1 OR wounded. 1 O.R. sick	

WAR DIARY or INTELLIGENCE SUMMARY

Army Form C. 2118.

1/4 K.A.L.I. Volume III 1st to 31st August 1918

Place	Date	Hour	Summary of Events and Information	Remarks and references to Appendices
OPPY SECTION	6/8/18		Dispositions changed. Commander TOMMY ALLEY inclusive & TIRED ALLEY inclusive. Instead of two coys in front line support and two in POST LINE, changed to one coy in front & support, two in POST LINE, and one about AIR PLANE POST. Move was completed by 10 a.m. Gas Bomb attack no injury to take place from Tommy Alley. From trench. 1 OR sick. 1 Rfn. ch. 2 OR sick.	B.
do	7/8/18		Gas Boom attack ordered for 2 a.m. Front trenches were evacuated accordingly. Attack cancelled at 2.5 min. to 2 and trenches reoccupied.	
do	8/8/18		Enemy artillery slightly more active throughout the day, especially on BAILLEUL and Tommy Alley Post trench strongpoints. 1 OR killed, 1 OR wounded, sick, 1 OR killed. From trench 3 OR sick on roster.	
do	9/8/18		Very quiet day. Relieve patrols as usual at night. 1 OR sick. To hosp. 1 Officer (2Lt Sanderman) and 2 OR sick from trenches. 1 OR sick. Cpl BOYD and Normal. Relieve patrols had nothing to report. 2 ORs. Returns 2 OR To trsp. Sick 3 OR	
do	10/8/18		Normal day. Few artillery rather more active in Embankment. A Tpt Sgt was evacuated out at 10 pm. From Hosp Sick 4 OR. To Hosp. Sick 3 OR. To Trans 1 OR.	
—	11/8/18		At 3 A.M. SqS Sgnl rounded up 15 repair of line Peter as barrage came down on 1 cm front at 2.9 AM Lasted for 20 minutes. No enemy attack delivered by small bodies patr'ls. At 9 relieved. A by in the outpost line. The disposition as eight in the outpost line are that 2nd Battn in concentrated on a front of not more than 600 to 700. Sus – 1 OR	

WAR DIARY / INTELLIGENCE SUMMARY

Army Form C. 2118.

1/7 H.L.I.   Volume III.   1st – 31st August 1918.

Place	Date	Hour	Summary of Events and Information	Remarks and references to Appendices
OPPY SECTION	12/8/18		A quiet day. Own artillery active as usual. To hospl. (sick) 1 O.R.	
"	13/8/18		The Battalion was relieved by the 6th H.L.I. and went into support. B, C & D Coys into BROWN LINE by BRIERLEY HILL TRENCH. Bn. H.Qrs. BRIERLEY. Bn-H.Qrs. BRIERLEY. Relief complete by midnight. From Hospl (sick) 1 OR, to	C
"	14/8/18		A quiet day. Own artillery active. Coys at work on trenches — and at musketry training. To Hospl (sick) 2 O.Rs.	
"	15/8/18		Quiet day. Normal artillery activity. C.O. relg. Commanding of 1st/5th Sherwood Foresters visited our preparatory to relief. Work on trenches & training continued. To Hospl (sick) 1 OR.	
"	16/8/18		A normal day. Bn. relieved by 1st/5th Sherwood Foresters. Relief from posts by 9 pm. "A" Coy marched to ROCLINCOURT, whilst conveyed by lorries to FRASER CAMP MONT ST. ELOY. Bn. trans [?] during movements from Hospl (sick) 2 OR. To Hospl 7 ORs wounded (gas) sick 3 OR. Bn. in bivouac at 2 pm — marched to MARQUEFFLES CAMP in CH. de la HAIE area — arrived in camp at 5 pm. Troops comfortably billetted in huts. To Hospl (sick) 2 OR.	D
MONT ST. ELOY	17/8/18			
MARQUEFFLES CAMP	18/8/18		Troops spent day cleaning up. C.O. in reconnaissance with B.G.C. Sidearts trained at night — by enemy planes. To Hospl (sick) 1 O/R. Captain W. F. TODD.	
"	19/8/18		Platoon training carried out. Coy. Commanders reconnoitred positions to be taken up in case of alarm. Joined Hospl (sick) 2 ORs. 2 ORs from reinforcements. 1 O/R. r/c T. A. PETRIE.	

WAR DIARY or INTELLIGENCE SUMMARY

Army Form C. 2118.

1/7th H.L.I.

Volume III.

1st – 31st August 1918.

Place	Date	Hour	Summary of Events and Information	Remarks and references to Appendices
MARQUEFFLES CAMP	20/8/18		Platoon training continued – Musketry, bayonet fighting, returns & drill – Bn in gas instruction – Bns paraded at 10.15 p.m. & marched (5 coys) near AIGNEZ LES DUISANS – arriving there about 3.30 a.m. – Remainder B in Nissen huts – Bn to β Platoon – Bn to Hosp (sick) 3.0 p.m. (Sick) 3.0 p.m. Reinforcement ¼ M. ROSS + 1 O.R. To Hosp (sick) 7 a.m.	
AIGNEZ LES DUISANS	21/8/18		A very hot day – men cleaning up & resting. Bn standing by ready to move at ½ an hour's notice – Enemy planes very active at night – bombing in vicinity of camp – 2 bombs falling in camp 3 O.R. killed & officers & 8 O.R. wounded. To Hosp (sick) 2 ORs.	
— do —	22/8/18		Coys at training in morning. All officers attended lecture on "Tanks" followed by Operations with infantry by G.S.O. II France. Tanks – Bn standing by to move at ½ an hour's notice parade at 11.15 p.m. marched to BELLACOURT arriving there at 3 a.m. and billeted in houses and tents. From Hosp (2 ORs) killed 1 Other. 2/Lt A.D. GALBRAITH. To Hosp (sick) 5 ORs.	
BELLACOURT	23/8/18		Bn paraded at 4 p.m. marched to Reception Camp near FICHEUX village. C.O. Reg. Commanding went ahead & arrived earlier. Bn very comfortably billeted in tents & huts. Coys given morning parade. Capt Am BLAIR struck off strength – assumed command 15th infantry in reserve. To Hosp (sick) 5 ORs.	
FICHEUX	24/8/18		Extra ammunition & bombs etc. issued at 7 a.m. and moved from to Trenches – The 157th Inf Bde. w/5th & 6th H.L.I. in front lines 157th Bde. in support. We captured 15 village & terrain this attack from the HINDENBURG LINE. Bn started at 7 a.m. at 5 a.m. & on passing Regt. suttlery & mines – (Stream Sba Shew France 5.16 S.W) depth meeting formation about 1½ miles in rear of 6 H.L.I. whereon attacking on IS right W/16 6 & 7 H.L.I.	

WAR DIARY
INTELLIGENCE SUMMARY

Army Form C. 2118.

1/7th H.L.I.   Volume III   1st – 31st August 1918.

Place	Date	Hour	Summary of Events and Information	Remarks and references to Appendices
	24/8/18 (continued)		In front Bty on right B Coy on left followed by A Coy on rt. C on left. The ground was difficult to the men. their advance owing to MG trenches mire. Fairly good progress was made. In spite of shelling from A.2.S. Direction was somewhat lost & Bn got N.E. of HENIN village almost to N32 b & N33 a. when it was held up by heavy machine gun fire - rebels [illegible] then Bn came to again further in vicinity of N26. At moved in small parties across valley of COJEUL River to sunken road at about T3 b. C. T24 c. a good many casualties occurred from MG fire during this movement. The Bn was then re-organised in C26 & 2 coys in sunken rd. in T3 B & T4 c. & 2 coys T4 C & T3 c & d. There positions were maintained throughout the afternoon. Later B Coy was moved up to about S[?]14 a. The other two left flank. Taking up positions in T3 a. Considerable shrapnelling was experienced. Throughout the afternoon strong & attempted movements brought up m.g. fire. Killed 10 O.Rs Lt T.W. PULLAR, R Wd. 3 ORS To Hosp(Wd) 2 O.Rs Wd: 3 --- Lt J. STRACHAN Wt 94 ORS Lt M. ROSS Hmiz 19 ORS Lt J.H. PETRIE Throughout the day the enemy [illegible] artillery (5.9s & T.25 & 177 ms) machine gun were active -- After dark B Coy was withdrawn from its front position along with A.B. & D Coy were deployed along sunken road in T3 B C & d. A.B. & D Coy in further road in T3 b N26 in withdraw all traps formed of sunken rd. in T3 a rc. recommencing C by one with each per to the road. This was done preparatory to a bombardment of heavy artillery for	
New HENIN 25/8/18			JAUSENBORG LINE. Wd(Sus) 1 Offr. W.R.E.R. MUIR. To Hosp(ilm) 2 ORS	

JAUSENBORG LINES
Wd(Sus) 1 Offr. W.R.E.R. MUIR.
Lgd   12 ORS
TO Hosp(ilm) 2 ORs

WAR DIARY or INTELLIGENCE SUMMARY

Army Form C. 2118.

1/7th H.L.I. Volume III. 1st – 31st August

Place	Date	Hour	Summary of Events and Information	Remarks and references to Appendices
Near HENIN.	24/8/18		Position maintained throughout the day. Patrols were sent out in afternoon following:— 2/Lt McCALLUM went with HENIN HILL with a view to establishing posts there to keep in touch with troops on our right. Lt. MILLER reconnoitred HINDENBURG LINE about N.34.a.r.c, got in touch with 15th R.S. (who today attacked down Eastline) + obtained useful information. a 2/Lt BUDDEFORD took another patrol to HENIN HILL to further reconnoitre HINDENBURG LINE — but could not procure any of Plans + M.G. Fire. Frontage (lion) (6.0.P.M.) W.J. McMahon Major KAEIK MILLER Reinforced 1/7th HLI to be drawn.	
	27/8/18		About 6 A.M. in due relief from Battn's attack to take HINDENBURG LINE, then advance to FONTAINE CRUISILLES and issues to take RIENCOURT. 6/HLI attacking on right, 7th on left with 5/HLI in reserve and mopping up — The Battalion's jumping off place was astride 15th/HINDENBURG LINE. + attack was timed at 9.20am. Considerable opposition was experienced during advance to jumping-off place from machine gun. shelly + trench mortar picking them way through dense belts of barbed wire under machine gun advance was continued — men B Co + No 2 line there. On my 6th being held up at the commencement, the attack for rattoon back on the trenches which went forward as 15th Coy + hr under last proponents made many prisoners while last of 15th on its right. On unwounded shortly then 24/b 5.w. of FONTAINE CRUISSILLES at midday. Then their further advance to last objective was organised. B. & Coys forged through trenches + were kept right away from the attack. B + B Coys found themselves in front of HINDENBURG LINE. there advanced lines frequently, A.R.G. Approach was met down HINDENBURG LINE. Many machine guns S.E. from about front — U.7.d. 8.5 — directed on RIENCOURT. Heavy machine gun	

WAR DIARY
INTELLIGENCE SUMMARY

Army Form C. 2118.

1/7th L.I.   Volume III.   1st – 31st August 1918.

Place	Date	Hour	Summary of Events and Information	Remarks and references to Appendices
	27/8/18 (continued)		Wm Robinson. Lnce/Corpl. renstate. Troops could not make progress. Though every endeavour was made to do so by some of the platoons. My front-line Sergt A LYALL D.C.M. was killed when his party found itself under enemy machine gun communication. Lieutenant Wilson the youngest subaltern in the enemy thrills explained. Mr Tilley however arranged a further advance down to 3.30 p.m. This was however put 4.30 p.m., but otherwise no orders than could not be obtained. Returns were also returned. playing trench mortars. shelling was considerable. The O.C. surrendered at night by O.C. 9th Bn King's Liverpool Regt. Killed Capt SEYMOUR - Q.L.I. killed 27 O.R.s M.C. Captn E MULLEN M.C. Wd. O.R.s 133. Lt. L.A. WOODBURN — M. Capt. W.H. McCALLUM — A. CAMPBELL. Capt. A. HORTON R.A.M.C.(att.) Wd. A.S. BARLOW (gas) To JOYRE (SICK) 5. O.R.s — G. O.R.s to	
	28/8/18		Reinforce carried out at 3 A.M. + Bn withdrew to Reservefoss. 9. O.R. 9 O.R. MERCATEL arriving there about midday. from troops (sick) 2. O.R. to " 9. O.R.	
	29/8/18		Bn resting. Re-organisation carried out. wiring + Camelia out company found into his HQs vown. A runner from Bn HQ to/from their last commander-in-Chief advised A. I.P.6. attached his handy Transfer to every officer. Bn Commander — on Reinforcements 3 officers — Lt. I.R.S. MUIR. Wd. to Troops Sick 11. O.R. Wd. I. CRAWFORD to " 1. O.R. Wd. D. McINNES.	
	30/8/18		A quiet day. Resting. Enemy planes active at night. Bombing in vicinity of camp. To troops (sick) 2. O.R.	

Army Form C. 2118.

WAR DIARY
or
INTELLIGENCE SUMMARY.
(Erase heading not required.)

Volume IV

1st – 31st August 1918.

1/7th H.L.I.

Instructions regarding War Diaries and Intelligence Summaries are contained in F. S. Regs., Part II. and the Staff Manual respectively. Title pages will be prepared in manuscript.

Place	Date	Hour	Summary of Events and Information	Remarks and references to Appendices
	31/8/18		On receiving Army instructions re new organisation – From Hopes (W.E.) - 1. O.R. To " Gun - 2. O.R.	

Summary of Casualties &c. for August 1918.

	Increase				Decrease			
	O/rs.	O.Rs.	Total.		O/rs.	O.Rs.	Total.
From Hospital (Sick)	1	81	82	To Hospital (Sick)	2	67	69
" " (W.)	–	1	1	" (W.)	9	249	258
Draft Reinforcements	68	3	11	Struck off Effective Strength	1	–	1
				" " " "	1	–	1
				Killed in action	5	58	63
				Missing: Failed to report after action.	–	23	23
Total	70	85	94	Total.	17	398	415

From Hospital (Sk.)
Capt. L. Bryson.
Struck-travel for Sgt.
2/Lt. O.R. Petrie   10/8/18.
" W. Ross   20/8/18.
" R. Brown   26/8/18.
Lt. G.R.L. Muir   }
2/Lt. I. Crawford   } 29/8/18.
2/Lt. D. McTaggart }

Officers L.t.B. in action
2/Lt. N.D. Balmain - 22/8/18.
2/Lt. J.H. Pollar - 24/8/18.
Capt. S.F. Gordon.
2/Lt. A. Morton- R.A.M.S. 29/8/18
2/Lt. O.H. McCallum

Officers W.d. in action
2/Lt. J.J. Strachan (slight) 24/8/18
2/Lt. W. Ross 24/8/18
2/Lt. O.R. Petrie 24/8/18
Lt. R.E.R. Muir 25/8/18

2/Lt. S.M. SANDEMAN
Officers St. to Hospital
Capt. W.J. Ivens 15/8/15
Struck off Effective Strength.
Capt. A. McFarlane
Command 52nd Div. Reption Bn.

[signature]
Lt Col. Comg. 1/7 H.L.I.

Copy No. 9

1/7TH. BN. HIGHLAND LIGHT INFANTRY.   MOVE ORDERS.

By Major H. Watson, M.C., Commanding.   1/9/16.

"A"

Ref. Map, Sheet 36 S. W. N. 1/20,000.

1. 157th. Infantry Brigade will relieve portions of 10th. Canadian Infantry Brigade and of 155th. and 156th. Infantry Brigades in the line to-day.

2. Brigade boundaries will be as follows:-
   (i) On the North. ELIHU ALLEY (inclusive to 155th. Inf. Bde.)
   (ii) On the South. B.33.a.9.7. - B.33.a.0.8. - B.32.b.5.0. - B.32.d.6.5. - B.31.c.0.0. - B.31 central - along North side of GAUL ALLEY (inclusive to 156th. Inf. Bde).
   (iii) Inter Battalion Boundary. TOMMY ALLEY (inclusive to 7th. H.L.I.

3. 7th. H.L.I. will be Left front Battalion, and will take over from 44th. Canadian Infantry Brigade, with Bn. Hqrs. at B.15.c.8.2.
   5th. H.L.I. will be Right front Battalion, Headquarters at B.21.a.0.5.
   5th. A.L.I. will occupy BROWN line within Brigade boundaries, with Battalion Headquarters at B.19.a.95.30.

4. The relief will be carried out by day, 7th. H.L.I. using PLANK ROAD and TIRED ALLEY. A distance of 200 yards will be maintained between platoons, which will move in sections. Guides from 44th. Canadian Battalion will meet platoons at end of PLANK ROAD at Debussing Point at 0800.

5. Dispositions will be :
   B. Coy. :- Right front Coy.
   C. Coy. :- Left front Coy. with ARMAGH ROAD inclusive to it.
   Both Companies occupy ROW TRENCH and ROW SUPPORT.
   Two platoons in ROW TRENCH and two platoons in ROW SUPPORT.
   A. Coy. :- Right rear Coy.
   D. Coy. :- Left rear Coy.
   Both Companies occupy POST TRENCH and trenches in that vicinity.

6. All Trench Stores, Aeroplane Photos, Maps, Work in hand and Work projected will be taken over.
   Companies will take over dispositions suggested by O.C. 44th. Canadian Battalion, meanwhile.

7. In the event of an alarm or enemy attack during the relief troops will man nearest defences, reporting dispositions at once to nearest Brigade Headquarters.

8. 157 Infantry Bde. will close at present site at 1500 to-day and open at same hour at A.32.a.4.5.

9. Coys. will enbus at Headquarters here commencing with B. Coy. at 0815, then C., D., A., H.Qs.
   all Lewis Guns and S.A.A. Magazines will be carried, also to-days rations and sufficient dixies to provide meals during the day.

10. Administrative Instructions will be issued later.

R. Strachan
Lieut. & A/Adjt.
1/7th. Bn. H.L.I.

SECRET.   COPY No. 6

TO :

Reference Secret Battalion Order dated 5/8/18, the NORTHERN BOUNDARY of the Battalion has changed, and will now run B.10.b.6.9. down the new un-named extension of TIRED ALLEY leading from PLUMER EXTENSION to YUKON, thence down TIRED ALLEY as far as its junction with the GREEN LINE. (The whole inclusive to the LEFT Brigade (155th.) and thence due WESTWARDS.

J. Strachan
Lieut. & A/Adjt.,
1/7th. Bn. H.L.I.

7/8/18.

SECRET.
Copy No. 6.

1/7th (Blythswood) Battalion - The Highland Light Infantry.

B A T T A L I O N   O R D E R S
By Lieut-Colonel E.S. Gibbons, D.S.O., Commanding.

5th August, 1918.

1. The Inter BATTALION BOUNDARIES are altered as follows:-
SOUTHERN BOUNDARY, TOMMY ALLEY (inclusive to Right Battn)
NORTHERN BOUNDARY, from B.10b.6.9. along TIRED ALLEY to its junction with BROWN LINE (inclusive to 157 Brigade) - TIRED ALLEY (inclusive to 155 Brigade) as far as its junction with GREEN LINE then due WEST.

2. The following alterations in Dispositions will take place tomorrow commencing after Breakfast and will be completed by 6p.m.

    A. Coy. will hold BOW TRENCH and BOW SUPPORT TRENCH SYSTEM taking over from B. & C. Companies, with 8 PLATOONS in BOW TRENCH and 2 PLATOONS in BOW SUPPORT TRENCH.

    B. Coy. will take over POST LINE FROM TOMMY ALLEY (exclusive to B10c0.0.)

    D. Coy. will hold POST LINE from B10c0.0. to TIRED ALLEY inclusive, with posts in LEEDS POST and CLYDE ALLEY near junction with TIRED ALLEY.

    C. Coy. will take over AIRPLANE POST SYSTEM from junction of AIRPLANE SWITCH and JIMMY TRENCH B.15b50.60. to TIRED ALLEY inclusive, holding JIMMY TRENCH and AIRPLANE SWITCH N. & S. of JIMMY TRENCH.

3. Completion of moves to be reported to Battn. Hdqrs. by Code Word "SPORT".

4. O.C. Companies will forward by 2p.m. 6th inst. a rough sketch showing new Dispositions.

5. ACKNOWLEDGE.

No. 1 Copy to A. Coy.
    2   B.
    3   C.
    4   D.
    5   C.O.
    6.& 7 War Diary.
    8   I.O.

Capt.
For Adjt. 1/7th Bn. H.L.I.

SECRET.   Copy. No. 6.

17th (Blythswood) Battalion - The Highland Light Infantry.

B A T T A L I O N   O R D E R S.

By Lieut-Colonel L.L. Gibbons, Commanding.
                                                    th August, 1916.

-:-:-:-:-:-:-:-:-:-:-:-:-:-:-:-:-:-

1. The Inter Battalion Boundaries are altered as follows:-
   (Southern Boundary TOMMY ALLEY inclusive to Right Battalion)
   (Northern Boundary from HQrs. along TIRED ALLEY to its junction with CROSS LINE (inclusive to 47 Brigade) - TIRED ALLEY inclusive to (45 Brigade) as far as the junction with GREEN LINE then due WEST.

2. The following alterations in dispositions will take place tomorrow commencing after breakfast. It will be completed by 6p.m.
   "A" Coy. will hold B" TRENCH and ROW TWO OF TRENCH TOTAL taking over from "B" and "C" Companies, with two Platoons in BOW TRENCH and two Platoons in BOW-SHOW TRENCH.

   "B" Coy. will take over POST LINE from TOMMY ALLEY exclusive to BLOCK.

   "D" Coy. will hold POST LINE from BLOCK to TIRED ALLEY inclusive, with posts in BLOCK posts and OTHER ALLEY nearest junction with TIRED ALLEY.

   "C" Coy. will take over AIRPLANE POST TOTAL from junction in AIRPLANE NOTCH and FIRST TRENCH BLOCK. to TIRED ALLEY inclusive, holding JIMMY TRENCH and SOUTH NW - SWITCH N. W. of JIMMY TRENCH.

3. Completion of moves to be reported to Battn. Hdrs. by Code word "SORT".

4. O.C. Companies will forward by 2p.m. 6th inst. a rough sketch shewing new Dispositions.

5. ACKNOWLEDGE.

No. 1 Copy to A. Coy.
" 2   "   " B.   "
" 3   "   " C.   "
" 4   "   " D.   "
" 5   "   " O.C.
" 6   "   " War Diary.
" 7   "   " H.Q.

SECRET.   Copy No.

1/7th. Bn. THE HIGHLAND LIGHT INFANTRY.

By Lieut. Col. E. T. Gibbons, D.S.O., Commanding.
                                                           12/8/18.

1. The Battalion will be relieved by the 6th. Bn. H.L.I. in the left sub-sector on the 13th. August, 1918. On relief the Battalion will take over the same dispositions as those at present held by 6th. Bn. H.L.I.

2. If the Gas Beam Attack which is ordered to take place has not been carried out before the 13th. instant, all orders and instructions regarding the same will be handed over by Coys. to 6th. Bn. H.L.I.

3. Relief will be carried out as follows :-
A. Coy., 6th. H.L.I. will relieve D. Coy. 7th. H.L.I. and will move at 0900 via TOMMY ALLEY.
B. Coy., 6th. H.L.I. will relieve B. Coy. 7th. H.L.I. and will move at 0930 via TIRED ALLEY and POST TRENCH.
C. Coy., 6th. H.L.I. will relieve C. Coy. 7th. H.L.I. and will move at 0900 via AIRPLANE SWITCH.
D. Coy., 6th. H.L.I. will relieve A. Coy. 7th. H.L.I. and will move at 0930 via TIRED ALLEY and POST TRENCH.

4. GUIDES. One guide per platoon will be supplied by 7th. H.L.I. as under :-
D. Coy. at junction of BOW SUPPORT and TOMMY ALLEY at 0900.
B. Coy. at junction of POST TRENCH and TIRED ALLEY at 0930.
C. Coy. at junction of BROWN TRENCH and AIRPLANE SWITCH at 0900.
A. Coy. at junction of BROWN TRENCH and TIRED ALLEY at 0930.
    Platoon guides from 6th. H.L.I. will be supplied as follows -
5. For D. Coy. 7th. H.L.I. at junction of TOMMY ALLEY and BROWN TRENCH.
For B. Coy. 7th. H.L.I.   do.   do.   do.   do.
For C. Coy. 7th. H.L.I. at junction of AIRPLANE SWITCH and BROWN TRENCH.
For A. Coy. 7th. H.L.I. at junction of TIRED ALLEY and BROWN TRENCH.

6. Trench Stores, Log Books, Special Maps and Plans will be handed over and receipts taken.
List of stores etc. handed over and taken over in new area will be forwarded to Bn. Headquarters by 1000 on 14th. instant.
24 Lewis Gun magazines will be exchanged, 6 magazines per gun will be carried ; also all metal boxes, canvas buckets and web pouches.

6. All work in hand and projected will be handed over in writing.

7. Completion of relief when Coys. have taken over their new areas will be wired to Bn. Hqrs. by code-word "VENUS".

8. ACKNOWLEDGE.

                                        J. Strachan
                                        Lieut. & A/Adjt.,
                                        1/7th. Bn. H.L.I.

DISTRIBUTION.
Copy No. 1.   O.C. A. Coy.
         2.   B.
         3.   C.
         4.   D.
         5.   H.Qs.
         6.   Office.
         7.   O.C., 6th. H.L.I.
         8.   War Diary.
         9.   War Diary.

5. TRANSPORT for L.G. Magazines and Cooking pots will be at the following places after dark:-
   "A" Coy.- One limber at SPUR POST on THELUS ROAD B.14.a.
   "B" Coy.- One limber at junction of THELUS ROAD and embankment B15.a.1.4.
   "C" Coy.- One limber on CONCRETE ROAD at cross roads. B21.a.3.8.
   "D" Coy.- One limber   do.
   ONE limber for Orderly Room Boxes, Signalling & Medical Equipment will be at junction of THELUS ROAD & Embankment, B.15.a.1.4.

SECRET.

1/7th (Blythswood) Battalion - The Highland Light Infantry.

MOVE ORDERS. No. 3.

By Lieut-Colonel E.S. Gibbons, D.S.O., Commanding.

15th August, 1918.

~~INTRODUCTION.~~ in the OPPY Section

1. The 157th Infantry Brigade will be relieved by the 24th Infantry Brigade on the 16/17th August, 1918.
   The 1st Bn. Sherwood Foresters will relieve the 1/7th Bn. H.L.I. in support in BROWN LINE. Companies will be relieved by same lettered Coys. of Sherwood Foresters.
2. Guides will be at the undermentioned points at 6-45p.m. 16th Augt.
   A. and B. Coys. 1 Guide per Platoon and 2 per Bn. Hdqrs. at head of TIRED ALLEY. *(Detailed instructions follow)*
   C. and D. Coys. - 1 guide per Platoon at head of CUSH ALLEY
3. All log books, maps 1 & 1 photos, trench and area stores, will be handed over and 10000 20,000 receipts obtained. Lists of Stores handed over will be forwarded to the Adjutant by 1200 on the 17th inst.
4. Lewis Guns and 8 magazines per gun will be carried out- remaining magazines will be conveyed by Transport.
5. 2 Limbers and Maltese Cart will be on CONCRETE ROAD at CROSS ROADS in B.21a and 2 Limbers at SPUR POST on THELUS ROAD - B14a after dark. Remaining L.G. Magazines and Cooking pots of C. and D. Coys. and Orderly Room boxes, Signalling and Medical Equipment will be loaded on to Transport *~~Cancelled~~* Magazines and Cooking pots of A. and B. Coys. will be loaded on to Transport at SPUR POST under Company arrangements. Transport when loaded will proceed to FRASER CAMP and unload.
6. After relief, C. and D. Coys. will proceed via CUSH ALLEY & CONCRETE ROAD and A. and B. Coys. and Bn. Hdqrs. via TIRED ALLEY and PLANK ROAD to ROCLINCOURT, whence Buses will take Bn. on to FRASER CAMP MONT ST. ELOY - Lt. Watson will act as Embarking Officer.
7. In the event of an alarm or enemy attack during the relief, Coys. will halt and man the nearest defences. Bn. will then concentrate at Bn. Headquarters.
8. Major Watson, M.O., C.Q.M. Sgts. and Sgts. Beveridge and Low will report to representative at NEW BDE. HDQRS. WHITE HOUSE, ST. ELOY, at 3p.m. on 16th inst. to take over Camp.
9. All area Stores in FRASER CAMP will be taken over. List of same will be submitted to the Adjutant by 1200 on 17th inst.
10. Transport and Q.M. Parties to remain at present position in ECOIVRES.
11. Rations will be drawn as at present from SUPPLY DUMP at ECOIVRES.
12. Battn. Bounds will be marked by Batten. Boards. No N.C.O. or man will leave the Battn. Area without a pass and unless properly dressed with waist belt.
13. The Battn. will be on duty on 17th inst.
14. All Personnel of Bde. Pioneer Coy. and nucleus details all rejoin at MONT ST. ELOY on 17th inst. and they will be rationed up to and including 16th inst.
15. Completion of relief by 1st Battn. Sherwood Foresters will be notified to Battn. Headquarters by code word "BAHUT".

P. Strachan
Lieut. & A/Adjt.
1/7th Bn. H.L.I.

COPY No. 1. OC. A. Coy.
2. B.
3. C.
4. D.
5. HQ. Coy.
6. Q.M.
7. Transport Officer.
8. File.
9 & 10. War Diary.

7.I.
17 sheets

17th H. Batt. Vol 6
War Diary for September 1915.

Army Form C. 2118.

WAR DIARY
or
INTELLIGENCE SUMMARY.
(Erase heading not required.)

1/1st H.L.I.   1st – 30th September 1918.

Place	Date	Hour	Summary of Events and Information	Remarks and references to Appendices
NEAR MERCATEL	1/9/18		Bn. paraded at 7.0 a.m. and marched to HENIN HILL where it bivouacked in the HINDENBURG LINE. The usual nucleus was left behind. This proceeded under Major WATSON M.C. to 16 Divl. Reception Camp. The Bn. was in a new organisation (only transmitting of 2 Platoons per Company. This being only a Company amalgamation. — To Hospl (Sick) – 7 O.R. The recruiment ready to answer at moment's notice.	
HENIN HILL	2/9/18		Bn. paraded at 5.10 a.m. and marched to positions in the HINDENBURG LINE – in TUNNEL TRENCH & TRIBURG SUPPORT, which previous the Bn. had left on the 28th August. A portion moved up the new dug along the HINDENBURG LINE to TRIDENT & NEPTUNE Trenches. M.G. BULLECOURT where both received a few rounds of mixed during the night – A reconnaissance of night – 2. O.Rs was made by Company Officers. Reinforcement 25 O.R. To Hospl (wounded) — 2. O.R. Trans. Hospl 6 O.R. 2. O.Rs.	
HINDENBURG LINE. (N. of BULLECOURT)	3/9/18		Bn. paraded at 5.0 a.m. to move to carry out attack on PRONVILLE, QUEANT and HINDENBURG Line. to bayonette with assembled Bdes. moved via BULLECOURT – RIENCOURT & HINDENBURG (L) SUPPORT LINE in D.S.t. (Sht. FRANCE 57c.NE). Bn. received their perish of 63rd Division (L) away from 16 Corps PRONVILLE – QUEANT. Bn. advanced at 11.45 a.m. with part Coys in HINDENBURG LINE in D.16. Upper P.X. O.M. following them followed by 'A' Company. This party advanced from a dug-out on our left flank (by a man of 'A' Company – 5th H.L.I. on left from about D.17 central during the afternoon – disposition were slightly east. — 5th H.L.I. on left from about D.17 central WADDELL COPSE. 7th H.L.I. with A.C. Coys in front HINDENBURG Tunnel — D.16a. The 6th H.L.I. in MELBOURNE SPRINT Coys in rear HINDENBURG Trench. Corps Support – from our Company no information of the report – had moved on to the Bn. was in Corps Support – from our Company Cushy Dug-out area where the troops lay as nearly as night – normal PRONVILLE (0 cu) vicinity. War Caone 90 missing. To Hospl (wounds) 1. O.R. (Sick) 8 O.R.	

Army Form C. 2118.

WAR DIARY
or
INTELLIGENCE SUMMARY.
(Erase heading not required.)

1/7th H.L.I.   1st – 30th September 1918

Instructions regarding War Diaries and Intelligence Summaries are contained in F. S. Regs., Part II. and the Staff Manual respectively. Title pages will be prepared in manuscript.

Place	Date	Hour	Summary of Events and Information	Remarks and references to Appendices
New PRONVILLE	4/9/18		Bn. remained in same position – Some enemy shelling of area – A quiet day –	
— " —	5/9/18		A quiet day – normal enemy activity – To Hospl. 1 Officer (wounds) Capt + Q.M. J. RUSSELL – 7 O.Rs.	
— " —	6/9/18		Quiet day – Bn. Joined by Lieut. G. V. A. BAIRD.	
NEU CROISILLES	7/9/18		At the move off Limbers at 6.00 – 4 mounted took to bivouac S.W. of CROISILLES – arriving there about 9.45 a.m. Route via PRONVILLE – QUEANT – NOREUIL – ECOUST. The division is 3rd in Corps Support. Joined – Lieut. I. M. HENRY. To Hospl. (sick) – 2 O.R. Capts. GOLD & SYKES + 7 Rr. Lanarkshire (Fortingal) transferred to M.K.	
— " —	8/9/18		Bn. paraded for Divine Service – Remainder of day spent in cleaning up – cleaning relieving camping area & collecting scraps – from Hospl. 4 O.R.	
— " —	9/9/18		Collection of scraps – cleaning up area – Coy. inspection – & reorganisation – from Hospl. 4 O.Rs. Reinforcements 1 O.R.	
— " —	10/9/18		Platoon training. All officers N.C.Os. attended lecture & demonstration by an officer of 3 J.G. of Training Brigade – "A" Coy. supplied a platoon and Lt. Dr. MACKIE for the demonstration. Lecture of interest & informative, weather – a. a. a wind – frequent rain showers – From Hospl. 2 O.Rs.	
— " —	11/9/18		Rain and bad weather interfered considerably with Training – Release from command of 15th Brigade reinforcements to temporary attached of Mr Lieut. C.B. Smith from C.R.S. A.B.Y. from Hospl. 2 O.Rs.	Claude Adams Lt Col 1/7 HLI CO

WAR DIARY or INTELLIGENCE SUMMARY

Army Form C. 2118.

1/7th H.L.I. — 1st – 30th September 1918

Place	Date	Hour	Summary of Events and Information	Remarks and references to Appendices
Nr CROISILLES	1/9/18		Cold, wet & windy weather – Coys: firing on ranges & practicing L.G. firing – Coy: Commanding Officers meeting – took application and 10 voters reports – A. Pte Coy: Lewis gun teams carried out L.G. firing – Bombing instruction – Left for Hospl. Pt. 25 man T.A.O.R. army Hospl. 5th Reinforcements 20th Bn.	
— do —	13/9/18		Bn: carried out usual work from 9.30 to 12.30 and Company Commanders conference in afternoon. Army Hospl. 1 OR. R.E. No. 17th Batt. proceeded to base for transfer to Home Establishment	
— do —	14/9/18		Bn: paraded at 9.30am – for Brigade parade – The Corps Commander (Sir Charles FERGUSSON K.C.B. K.C.M.G. M.V.O. D.S.O.) addressed the Bn. & thanked all ranks for their work during the past operations – C.O. Company Commanders & Intelligence Officer visited the 1/4 S. Lancs Regt. of 172 Bde. in the line – prior to taking over — To Hospl. Sick 3 ORs	
— do —	15/9/18		The Bn: attended Divine Service in the afternoon. The Bde. received the following NCOs. from 9/58 Div. for gallantry & distinguished conduct during the past operations:— The Bn: received the Military Medals:– 281093 Sergt. P.B. SCOTT. 260984 L.Cpl. A. PORT. 280419 " J. JOHNSTON. 282087 Pte H. BENTLEY. 280474 Cpl. J. BEATTIE. 280837 " T. MURPHY. The following were also awarded the Military Medal, but were not present at the ceremony:— 280570 Sergt. J. GOODFELLOW. 281212 L.Cpl. E. FAIRMAN. 280115 Pte W. LEE. 280251 Pte W. ANDERSON. 280677 Cpl. J. MUIR. 281517 Pte W.A. PATTERSON. 281326 " W. McNAUGHT. Lt. Col. A.M. Bruce assumed duties Hospl. for Day – To Hospl. Sick 4 ORs Army Hospl. 1 OR	

Army Form C. 2118.

WAR DIARY
or
INTELLIGENCE SUMMARY.
(Erase heading not required.)

Instructions regarding War Diaries and Intelligence Summaries are contained in F. S. Regs., Part II. and the Staff Manual respectively. Title pages will be prepared in manuscript.

Place	Date	Hour	Summary of Events and Information	Remarks and references to Appendices
Nr. CROISILLES	16/9/18		Malins left at 1.30 under Captain Boyd preparatory to Divn Reception Camp. The Battn paraded at 2.40 p.m. marched to Ruins W. of QUEANT & stopped there for evening meal. At 7.30 Battn moved off by platoons & took over line at INCHY-en-ARTOIS from 2/4 Lancashire Regt. y relieving in support with 5th H.L.I Regt from 6th H.L.I. left as later in front. D Coy of the Battn was placed at disposal commander of 5th H.L.I from "B" Regt Hqrs 2/Lt as ready Sect to Hopl. 10v	A
INCHY-en-ARTOIS	17/9/18		Ref MAP SHEET 57C NW 112.0000. Enemy concentration reported at CANAL DU NORD in front of MOEUVRES. Our Artillery put down barrage about 1100. Enemy replied about 6.30 P.M. German patrols did some damage in our lines & attacked North MOEUVRES. our artillery replied with all available. Lt. J. R.G. Muir B Coy died of G.S.W received. Killed in Action :- 1 OR From Hopl & MG NN To Hopl Wounded in Action :- 6 OR died to Hopital 1 OR	
"	18/9/18		Day comparatively quiet. except for intermittent shelling by both sides. A number BLUE CROSS shells landed in the valley W. of INCHY. 2nd Lt "n. Cannoch" sick and 15th platoon moved up to SWAN LANE to commence station 154 & 155 Bdes Reinforcements :- 61 ORS From Hopl 4 ORs To Hopl Wounded in Action :- 14 ORs 3 ORs died to Hospital. 10v	

WAR DIARY
INTELLIGENCE SUMMARY
Army Form C. 2118.

(Erase heading not required.)

Place	Date	Hour	Summary of Events and Information	Remarks and references to Appendices
NEAR INCHY-en-Artois	19/9/18		Refmab. Sheet 39°NW 1:20000 C.O. & officers of 24th Canadian Infantry Regt. came up at G. 9.10 A.M. to reconnoitre line before taking over at night. Intermittent shelling by both sides throughout the day — usual gas shells in valley N of INCHY. C.O. went to Bde. H.Q. at 4.30 P.M. From which orders were received & given for A & C Coys to move up to HOBART TRENCH & B Coy to move down to A Coy front position. A & C Coys moved & commanded by 155° Bde. attacked under barrage at 7 P.M. & took objective CEMETERY SUPP. E14. N of MOEUVRES 155° Bde. taking MOEUVRES. Lt Col. E.L. Gibbons D.S.O. died of wounds in vicinity of the attack. He gave orders to A & C Coys before the attack at 7 P.M. & no definite information can be obtained as to whom he met — his death. Batt. HQ A & C Coys returned to bivouac by the 24th & 25th Canadian Inf. Regts. at 11.35 P.M. & proceeded to bivouac area at NOREUIL. /pv	C
			Killed in action ..... 1 OR To Hosp. Wounded. 25 ORs dic ORs Jto Hosp. 1 A. 17.13 To Hosp. sick	
Near NOREUIL	20/9/18		Day devoted to rest, cleaning up &c. Lt Col. E.L. Gibbons D.S.O. buried at QUEANT CEMETERY. Representative from 11th Brigade & personnel of the Bde. were present. Received orders than A & C Coys would be relieved during the night. ½hr. W.P. MacKie killed while commanding A Coy at CEMETERY SUPPORT /pv	Cas. Lt. Mate 25/9/18 4.17.21
			To Hosp. sick 2 ORs	

Army Form C. 2118.

WAR DIARY
or
INTELLIGENCE SUMMARY.
(Erase heading not required.)

Instructions regarding War Diaries and Intelligence Summaries are contained in F. S. Regs., Part II. and the Staff Manual respectively. Title pages will be prepared in manuscript.

Place	Date	Hour	Summary of Events and Information	Remarks and references to Appendices
Near NOREUIL	21/9/18		"A" & "C" Coys arrived battalion about 9 A.M from MOEUVRES. Day devoted to rest, reorganisation & cleaning up. Major C. Gibb came from 6th Bn R.S.T. & took command of Bn. Lieut. Woolcock & Capt. of 60 O.R. arrived under Capt. J. Boya from Div Reception Camp. Capt. Jenkins to hospital. To Hospital Sick - 1 Offr From Hospital 12 O.R.s	
"	22/9/18		Divine Service at 9.30 A.M. Battalion allotted baths at ECOUST from 1.30 P.M. to 4.30 pm. Lt J.M. Smith returned from leave 2/Lt Parker from Hospital & 2/Lt Bennie from U.K. To Hospital Sick 1 O.R. 16 N	
"	23/9/18		Battalion handed over for training to specialised training carried on under battalion coy. commanders. To Hospital Sick 5 ORs from Hospital 10 R. transferred to 10th R.S.I. 1 O.R. army Signal Sgt a Clerking to ask for promotion. To Hospital Sick 5 ORs	
"	24/9/18			

WAR DIARY or INTELLIGENCE SUMMARY

Army Form C. 2118.

Place	Date	Hour	Summary of Events and Information	Remarks and references to Appendices
Near NOREUIL	24/9/18		Ref. map 57ᶜ NW 1:20000 Lt Black took over command of "B" Coy from Lt Baird. Commanding Officer proceeded at 0920 to reconnoitre line with Battn. commanders. Battalion paraded at 1000 for C.O's inspection which was taken by Capt Pyle in his absence. One or two H.V. shells thrown about in vicinity of area during the day. To Hospital sick: 5 ORs. MN	
— " —	25/9/18		Training carried out under Coy arrangements from 0900 – 1230. Warning orders received for pending operations. Battn paraded at 1930 — marched to bivouac area W. of QUEANT. Rendezvous under Capt Pyle & transport moving in their present bivouac area. To Hospital wounded 1 OR from Shell. 2 ORs MN sick. 10 ORs " To G.O.C. Kenting & D.O (Gas) to M.P.R.E. bombing Sgt Major Rob. m.6. (1/32-2A) regarding his transport protection by Army demobilized. C.O.	D.
Near Queant	26/9/18		Orders for the battle received from Brigade 1020 C.O. & Coy held conference at 9am re moves to battle position. Coy commanders proceeded immediately would take S of MONCHRES. Orders received 2nd day 27th inst. C.O. held conference & gave battle orders to Capt. Butn paraded by coy, marched to the battle position at intervals of 4 hour. starting at 1900 B.D.C. 4 GRs. A rebooked address To Hospital Sick: 1 OR from Shell 1 OR Gassed... To Hospital Gassed... MN	

WAR DIARY or INTELLIGENCE SUMMARY

Army Form C. 2118.

Place	Date	Hour	Summary of Events and Information	Remarks and references to Appendices
Near MOEUVRES	27/9/18		Ref. Map 57C NW 1:20000	

Zero hour received given to Coys. Battle to open at 05:20. At 05:20 a magnificent barrage was put down by our artillery at zero + 15' minutes 'B' Coy moved forward to take ALF.TR. with very little opposition & made headway for CANAL DU NORD. Simultaneously C. & D. Coys formed up in battle formation mid South East for the CANAL & their objectives. A Coy remaining in reserve in WILLIS TRENCH. B Coy experienced some difficulty at the CANAL & took up a position on W bank owing to M.G. fire. They eventually got across & established posts on the E. Bank about 09:30. D Coy got straight to objective & established posts on E bank of CANAL - a little trouble was experienced from M.G. on CAMBRAI Rd which was eventually overcome. "C" were held up about 200x from their objective - part of the coy having been left at jumping off tape. coy was reorganized & went forward & took objective No 6 LOCK & established posts. The 34th Divn. went through going E about 09:30 - Coys reorganized & took up new dispositions ALT.TR. Northern boundary to COW ALLEY Southern boundary. Outposts E of CANAL in touch with 152 Bde. Capture: P. of War. 46 - Heavy MGs 2. Light MGs 14. ANTI TANK rifle 2. 2/Lt D. McClure. Wounded.
Lt J. m. Smith. Died of wounds.
O. Rks Killed 50. O.Rks wounded
14 Missing. M/R
4 Died of Wounds.

Army Form C. 2118.

WAR DIARY
or
INTELLIGENCE SUMMARY.

(Erase heading not required.)

Instructions regarding War Diaries and Intelligence Summaries are contained in F. S. Regs., Part II. and the Staff Manual respectively. Title pages will be prepared in manuscript.

Place	Date	Hour	Summary of Events and Information	Remarks and references to Appendices
S of MOEUVRES	28/9		Ref. Map 57cNW 1:20,000. Normal orders to-day received. Salvage work carried out throughout the day. To Bde. Sch. 3 ORs. from Bde. Sch. 8 ORs. SW	
"	29/9		About 8:30 Mechows arrived from Brim Roofton Camp under Capt. Lyle. 2nd Lts. Gordon, G. Haddock, L. Parr, & McTeadic joined from U.K. for duty. Battalion salvage & cleared area in vicinity of GRAINCOURT & ANNEUX. 2nd Lt. A.E. Walker from leave. To Bde. Sch. 2 ORs. SW	
"	30/9		Battn carried out salvage work & cleared area in the vicinity of N of MOEUVRES. Warning order received that batt. would probably move forward at an early hour on 1st Oct. To Bde. Sch. 3 ORs. from Bde. Sch. 2 ORs SW	[signature]

WAR DIARY or INTELLIGENCE SUMMARY.

Army Form C. 2118.

Instructions regarding War Diaries and Intelligence Summaries are contained in F.S. Regs., Part II. and the Staff Manual respectively. Title pages will be prepared in manuscript.

(Erase heading not required.)

Place	Date	Hour	Summary of Events and Information	Remarks and references to Appendices

Summary of Casualties &c for September 1918

Increase	Off.	O.R.	Total	Decrease	Off.	O.R.	Total
From Hospital (sick)	-	40	40	To Hospital (sick)	3	81	84
" (war)	1	17	18	" (war)	2	99	101
Draft Reinforcements	11	89	100	Struck off effective strength	3	-	3
				Killed in action	4	14	18
				To N.K. for Comnds.	1	3	3
				To B.a.m.T.C. (B.T. & S.A)	1	-	-
				Missing after action	1	8	8
Total	12	146	158	**Total**	12	206	218

From Hosp. Wounded
2/Lt. A.J. Vokes

Draft joined for Duty:
Lieut. J.M.A. Baird 6/9/18
" J.M. Henry 7/9/18
2/Lt. G.W. Brodie 13/9/18
" C.M. Moore 23/9/18
" T.G. Little 26/9/18
" G. Boal "

Officers Killed in Action
Lt-Col. D.L. Gilmore 19-9-18
2/Lt. J.W. Cochrane 19-9-18
2/Lt. J. Evans-Smith "

Died of Wounds
Major G. Bell from 5 Bn. Brigade Command from 29/9/18
Brigade command from 29/9/18
Joined Unit 29/9/18
2/Lt. J.S. Loudon "
" H.G. Haddock "
" G. Park "
" J.M. Brodie "

Wounded in Action
Capt. Russell 3/9/18
2/Lt Br Coulson 21-9-18
Lt Q.R.S Twist 19-9-18
" J.W. Lowe 28-9-18
Lt. A.S. Moir 12-9-18
2/Lt. A.S. Varty 16-9-16
Capt. A.S. J.G. Jenkins 21/9/18

SECRET

1/7th. H. L. I.   Battalion Orders No. 1.   19th Sept., 1918.

By Lieut. Col. E. S. Gibbons, D. S. O.   Commanding.

No. 1. After relief the 157th Infantry Brigade will withdraw to bivouac area between PRONVILLE and NOREUIL.

" 2. All trench stores and orders regarding defences will be handed over and receipts obtained.

" 3. On completion of relief companies will march off by platoons at 100 yards distance. Route - PRONVILLE, QUEANT and NOREUIL ROAD.

" 4. All Lewis Guns, Magazines, Cooking Utensils, Signalling and Medical Equipment; Mess Stores, Petrol Tins, &c., will be loaded on to limbers at the Ration Dump. 5 Limbers and the Maltese Cart will be at Ration Dump at 12 Midnight. Companies will leave small parties to load limbers and proceed with them to bovouac area.

" 5. Completion of relief will be wired PRIORITY to Battalion Headquarters by code word "TOPHOLE".

" 6. In the event of alarm or enemy attack during the relief, troops will man nearest defences and report disposition to Battalion Headquarters.

" 7. Acknowledge.

" 8. Quartermaster will arrange to have hot tea ready for Coys. on arrival at bivouacs area from 2 a.m.

(sd) W. Weir, Lt. & A/Adjt.
1/7th Bn. H. L. I.

Copy No. 1   A.
     2   B.
     3   C.
     4   D.
     5   H.Q.
     6   Q.M.
     7   War Diary (1)
     8 F 9 File (2).

1/7th. Bn. H.L.I.   MOVE ORDERS. No. 7.

By Lieut. Col. E. S. Gibbons, D.S.O., Commanding.

Reference Map Sheet 57 C N.E. 1/20,000.

The 157th. Infantry Brigade will relieve the 172nd. Infantry Brigade in the left section of the 59nd. Divisional Sector on the night of the 16th./17th. September, 1918.
5th. H.L.I. will relieve the 1st. Royal Munster Fusiliers in the front line right.
6th. H.L.I. will relieve the 9th. Kings' Liverpool in the front line left.
7th. H.L.I. will relieve the 2/4th. South Lancashire Regt. in Support.

Coys. will relieve same lettered Coys. of 2/4th. S. Lancs. Regt. in the following order from right to left :-
D., C., A., and B. Coys.
The Battalion will parade at 3.40 p.m. to-day. Dress :- Full marching order ; greatcoats in packs. Bn. will march via ECOUST - NOREUIL - QUEANT.
~~Battalies will hald~~ Distances of 300 yards between Battalions, and 100 yards between platoons and every four vehicles will be maintained on the march.
Battalion will halt West of QUEANT for the evening meal.
Battalion will not pass East of MELBOURNE STREET before 8 p.m.

GUIDES. Guides from 2/4th. S. Lancs Regt. will meet Bn. Hqrs. C. A. and B. Coys. at D.10.a.8.3. (where MELBOURNE STREET cuts the INCHY-PRONVILLE ROAD). Guides will meet D. Coy. at D.10.c.3.0., whence Battalion will proceed by following routes :
Bn. Hqrs. and B. Coy. via MELBOURNE STREET and HINDENBURG SUPPORTS.
C. and A. Coys. via track through D.10.b. and D.11.a. and B.
D. Coy. via track through D.10.d. ~~and D.17.a. and b, and D.18.a.~~

LEWIS GUNS AND MAGAZINES. Lewis Guns and Magazines will be conveyed by limber to halting place west of QUEANT, after which guns and 16 magazines per gun will be carried on the man. Remaining 14 magazines per gun will be conveyed to the line by limber.

GAS. Owing to danger of gas shelling during relief great care will be taken to conceal any extra movement by day-light, and platoons must not close up during the march.
In the event of an alarm or enemy attack during the relief Coys. will man the nearest defences, reporting their dispositions to Bn. Hqrs..
Bn. Hqrs. will be at D.5.c.60.65.
Completion of relief will be wired priority to Bn.HQs. by code word "BABA".
No time must be lost in getting into position as relieving Bn. must be out before daylight.
Receipts for trench shelters, petrol tins, all battle stores etc. taken over by Coys. will be handed in at Bn. Hqrs. by 8 a.m. on 17th. instant.

TENTS, SHELTERS. All tents, shelters in present area will be handed over to relieving Bn.

NUCLEUS. Nucleus will parade at 1.30 p.m. under Capt. BOYD and will march to Reception Camp at BOISLEAUX.

Lieut. & A/Adjt.,
1/7th. Bn. H.L.I.

16-9-18

SECRET.   COPY.

1/7th Bn.(Blythswood) Battalion.   The Highland Light Infantry.

O R D E R S.

By Lieut. Col. E. S. Gibbons, D.S.O.   Commanding.   19/9/18.

The Canadian Infantry Brigade relieves 157th Brigade in the INCHY Sector on the night of the 19/20 September, 1918.

25th Can. Infy. Bn. will relieve 5th H.L.I. and D.C. & A. Coys. 7th H.L.I.

26th Can. Infy. Bn. will relieve 6th H.L.I. and A. & D. Coys. 7th S.R. in BUISSY SWITCH.

24th Can. Infy. Bn. will relieve B. Coy. 7th H.L.I. in D.6.D. and B. & C. Coys. 7th S.R. in ADELAIDE STREET.

The 25th Can. Infy. Bn. will enter front line by track running through D.10.A. & B. & D. 11 A. & B.
24th & 26th Can. Infy. Bns. by HINDENBURG SUPPORT LINE and track running through D 4 C & D., D. 5 C. & D. (D. 6 C. & D.)

Order of relief. 5th H.L.I. 6th H.L.I. 7th H.L.I. and 7th S.R. 157th L.T.M.B.

ADVANCE PARTIES.

A guide detailed from H.Q. 7th H.L.I. will meet advance party of unit of 5th Can. Infy. Bde. at PRONVILLE in street at D.2 B. Central at 8 A.M. this morning, 19th inst., and conduct this advance party to Bn. H.Q.

Guides for the evening at the rate of 4 per platoon (i.e. 4 per Coy) and 2 for Bn. H.Q. will meet incoming units as follows:-
A. Guides from B. Coy. and BN. H.Q. 7th H.L.I. for 24th Infy. Bn. and Guides from A. & D. Coys 7th S.R. for 26th Can. Infy. Bn. will be at D. 9 B. Central (PRONVILLE) at 7:30 p.m.

2nd Lt. M'Innes will be in charge of these guides.
B. Guides from C.D. & A. Coys. for 25th Can. Infy. Bn. and Guides from B! & C. Coys. 1/7th S.R. for Coys. of 24th Can. Infy. Bn, will be to D 9 B 51 (N.W. end of PRONVILLE) at 7:30 p.m.

2nd Lt. Brown will be in charge of these guides. The roads and way into the line will be previously reconnitred by the officer in charge and guides.

Guides for (a) above will report to 2nd Lt. M'Innes at Bn. H.Q. at 9.30 a.m. to-day to reconnoitre route.

Guides for (b) above except B. & C. Coys. 7th S.R. will report to 2nd. Lt. Brown at D.12 B.60.0 at 9.30 a.m. B. & C. Coys. 7th S.R. will join party where road crosses ADELAIDE STREET at D.11B.8.0

These Guides are to move in small parties.
Officers in charge of guides will arrange meeting place for guides for evening relief.

Lieut. & A/Adjt.
1/7th BN, H. L. I.

SECRET   M O V E   O R D E R.   Copy No.

1/7th (Blythswood) BN.   Highland Light Infantry.

                    B A T T A L I O N   O R D E R S.   25th Sept., 1918

By Major C. Gibb   Commanding.

257th Infantry Brigade less 5th H.L.I. and 157th L.T.M.B.
will move this evening to Bivouac Area about D. 27.

STORES.   Bivouacs will be rolled in bundles of five and stacked at
          Quartermasters Store at 1730.
          Tents, Officers Valises and Company Stores will also be
          returned at that hour.
          "C" Company will detail loading party of one N.C.O. and
          twelve men to report to Quartermaster at 1730.
          Battalion will parade ready to move off at 1800. 1930

ORDER OF MARCH.   Headquarters, A, B, C, & D.

          Platoon distance of 100 yards will be maintained throughout the
          march.

                                              Lieut. & A/Adjt.
                                              1/7th Bn. H.L.I.

1/7th (Blythswood) Battalion – The Highland Light Infantry.

COPY NO:- 1

MOVE ORDERS No. 3.
By Major C. Gibb ....Commanding.,

30th Septr. 1918

-:-:-:-:-:-:-:-:-:-:-:-:-:-:-:-:-:-:-

REFERENCE SHEET:-57c N.E.

1. The 157th Infantry Brigade will move EAST tomorrow and take over the Line from the 63rd Division in F30 and be in support to 155 Inf. Bde.,

2. 5th H.L.I. will be on the right; 6th H.L.I. on Left and 7th H.L.I., in reserve.

3. (1) Order of March commencing 1400:-
      6th H.L.I.,
      5th H.L.I.,
      7th H.L.I.,
      157th L.T.M.B.,
Starting Point:- CAMBRAI ROAD CANAL CROSSING E 27c 1:3! 500 yd distance will be maintained between Bns. and 100 yds between Coys
(11). 7th H.L.I., will parade at 1400. Each Coy. at its present bivouac in readiness to march on the signal being given; when Coys. will move forward and gain their correct order and distances.
    Order of March .... Hd. Qrs. Coy.
            A. Coy.
            C. Coy.
            D. Coy.
            B. Coy. Lewis Guns and S.A.A. Wagons and Maltese Cart.

4. The Commanding Officer and Coy Commanders will meet the B.G.C. at CANAL CROSSING E27 c1.3. mounted and accompanied by grooms at 1100.

5. The I.O. will meet the Bde. I.O., mounted, at CANAL CROSSING E27 c1.3 at 0900 tomorrow to proceed in advance to reconnoitre L'ESCAUT CANAL and RIVER CROSSINGS, and best route from EAST of CANTAING.

6(1) Limbered G.S. Wagons carrying Lewis Guns and S.A.A. also Maltese Cart will accompany Battalions. The remaining Transport, i.e. Field Kitchens, Water Carts, tool Carts and baggage wagons will march under the orders of the Staff Captain after all Units have passed the Starting Point, in same order of march as Units (viz. 6th, 5th, 7th H L I.)
(11) Transport of 7th H L I., will draw up on Road running through E26d with head of Column clear of main CAMBRAI ROAD, ready to move off at 1430.

7. A hot meal in Cookers will be ready for men when transport arrives at the new area.
8. Nucleus will remain at Battalion Transport Lines and not return to Divisional Reception Camp.
9. Rations will be issued on arrival at new Transport Lines.

10. Water Carts will move full. Water has been ordered for 12 noon to enable this to be done.
11. Greatcoats will be carried on the man in the pack. (If leather Jerkins are issued before off they will be ~~dumped~~ also carried in the pack and not worn).

12. Tents and Trench shelters will be dumped at Bn. Hd. Qrs by 1230 the shelters being rolled in bundles of five.
13. Midday meal will be at 1200.

Copy. No. 1. Hd Qrs. Coy.
      2 A. Coy.
      3 B. Coy.
      4 C. Coy.
      5 D. Coy.
      6 Q.M.
    7 & 8 War Diary.
      9. Office File.

LIEUT. & A/ADJT.
1/7th Bn. H.L.I.

ISSUED
BY
AT
ON.

7th Batt. H.L.I.

War Diary for Month of October 1915

WAR DIARY
or
INTELLIGENCE SUMMARY.

(Erase heading not required.)

Army Form C. 2118.

Place	Date	Hour	Summary of Events and Information	Remarks and references to Appendices
West MOUVRES	1/10/18	Ref Map 57c NE 1:20,000	Orders for move received at 0830, morning spent in preparation. Battalion paraded at 1400 marched off, coys at 100x distance, route VIA GRAINCOURT & CANTAING. Nucleus under Major Walkin remained at GRAINCOURT. Battalion took over — as battalion in reserve — from the "HAWKE" BATTN. (63RD DIVN) in T20 C. Slight intermittent shelling of area during the night. 2/Lt W.T. Vallance died of wounds 29/9/18. To Hosp. sick 5 OR. From hospl. 1 OR	BATTN ORDER NO 3
West CANAL DE L'ESCAUT T.30.c.	2/10/18		Light shelling in vicinity of area. Men employed deepening trenches for defensive purposes. To hospital 2 OR from hospl 2/Lt W. WORLEY. Reinforcements 8 OR & LTS R.W CANNING, T.W. McLEAN. R. PATON	
"	3/9/18		Cleaning up & deepening of trenches. Bttn. paraded at 1930 under Capt LYLE + under orders of a pioneer officer, proceeded forward to 153" Bde area to dig a communication trench. Blue cross shells frequently used on our area during the night. To hospital wounded 1 OR. From hospital sick 4 OR. To hospl. 2nd Lt. J. Crawford	

Army Form C. 2118.

WAR DIARY
or
INTELLIGENCE SUMMARY.
(Erase heading not required.)

Ref. map 57c NW 1:20000

Place	Date	Hour	Summary of Events and Information	Remarks and references to Appendices
NEAR CANAL DE L'ESCAULT F.30.C	4/10/18		Battalion returned from digging parade at 0400 & served with a hot meal. Orders received for relief of 13th Bde. in the line. Battalion moved at 1930 hours & effected the relief, taking over area from 6th H.L.I. in F.30.a. Move reported complete at 2100. To hospital 12 O.R. From hospital 3 O.R. Reinforcements 1 O.R. Lt A W PHILIP taken on strength Actg. B.M. sowers	
" F.30.A	Z/M.O.R.S 4/10/18 5/10/18		Intermittent shelling in vicinity of area throughout the day. Major FOSTER took over command of the battn. from Major GIBBS, the latter proceeding to take command of the 4th R.S.F. Battalion relieved by the 9th Kings (57th Divn) & proceeded to area previously occupied, S of MOEUVRES on W bank of CANAL DU NORD. To hospital wounded 1 O.R. To hospital sick 2 O.R. 2/Lt. J M°CALLUM D.C.M. for duty. 1 O.R. to 4th R.S.F.	
NEAR MOEUVRES	6/10/18		Day devoted to rest & cleaning up. Inclement under Major WATSON rejoined the battalion. Warning order received that battalion would entrain on the 7th inst. From L.T.M.B. 3 O.R. Reinforcements 3 O.R. To hospl. sick 2 O.R. From hospital sick 5 O.R. at Wei. Wnd. 4 O.R	

Army Form C. 2118.

WAR DIARY
or
INTELLIGENCE SUMMARY.
(Erase heading not required.)

Place	Date	Hour	Summary of Events and Information	Remarks and references to Appendices
Near MOEUVRES	7/10/18		Ref. Map 57e 1:20000. Orders received 0330 issued to coys 0820. Morning devoted to preparations. Battn. paraded at 1400 marched to VAULX–VRACOURT arriving 1800 entrained at 1930 the train moving off at 2025. From Hospl. Sick 3 O.R.s.	BATTN. ORDERS No 5
PETIT HOUVIN & LIENCOURT	8/10/18		Ref Map 51C 1:40000. Arrived at PETIT HOUVIN at 0830 & detrained. Battn paraded & moved off about 0915 to LIENCOURT, arriving at 1300. Afternoon devoted to settling in billets. 2/Lt R.M. Croft 2/Lt L.J. Dugno Joined unit for duty.	
LIENCOURT	9/10/18		Day devoted to cleaning up & making out heads of reference. C.O's conference re-programme of training, during period of stay in area. Lt S. Maitland Hogh. Capt of Telegh-Shore. 2/Lt D.S. Mitchard 2/Lt J. Fair 2/Lt J. Kinnear Joined Unit for duty. From Hospl. Wounded 3 O.R.s. Reinforcement 4 O.R.s.	
"	10/10/18		Slight rain. Organisation of Platoons. from 0900–1200 & 1400–1500. C.O's address to Battalion officers. 2/Lt J.E. Campbell Joined unit for duty. From Hospl. Wounded 1 O.R. Sick 3 O.R.s	

WAR DIARY
or
INTELLIGENCE SUMMARY.

Army Form C. 2118.

Place	Date	Hour	Summary of Events and Information	Remarks and references to Appendices
LIENCOURT	11/18		Ref Map 51C 1/40000	
			Platoon training under coy arrangements. Weather dull. "A" by Range practice on "F" Range 125:A. C.O.'s orderly room & coy Commdrs conference. 1400. 2 O.R.s to Hosp. (sick)	Joined its
"	12/10/18		Platoon training under coy arrangements. C.O's orderly room. Coy Commdrs conference at 1480. Weather dull. 2/Lieut J.A. PETRIE to Hosp. (sick) 1 O.R. to Hosp. Sk. 5 O.R.s from Hosp. 1 O.R. from Base. 1 O.R. to 157 L.T. Mg. Bn.	Weather dull
"	13/10/18		Divine service 0900. C.O.'s inspection of billets etc 1100. From Hosp. 8 O.R.S. From Base 1 O.R.	Weather
"	14/10/18		Platoon training under coy arrangements 0900 - 1200. "B"Coy Range practice on "E" Range 125:A 0830 - 1000. "C"Coy Range Practice 1000 - 1130. Lecture to officers & N.C.O's at 1330 by Lt Col James R.A.F. in "Le Chateau" GRANVILLECOURT. Night operation carried out by coys from 1920 - about 2200 Lt Hosp Sect 4 O.R. Capt & Quartermaster T. BOYCE joined unit for duty.	
"	15/10/18		Platoon training under coy arrangements 0900 - 1200 1400 - 1500 Weather dull From Base 4 O.R.s From Hosp. 4 O.R.S.	

Army Form C. 2118.

WAR DIARY
or
INTELLIGENCE SUMMARY.

(Erase heading not required.)

Instructions regarding War Diaries and Intelligence Summaries are contained in F. S. Regs., Part II. and the Staff Manual respectively. Title pages will be prepared in manuscript.

Place	Date	Hour	Summary of Events and Information	Remarks and references to Appendices
LIENCOURT	16/10/19		Ref map Sheet 51.C 1/40000 Platoon training under Coy arrangements from 0900 – 1300 1400 – 1500 Platoon tactical schemes carried out. Sick to Hosp. 5 ORs from Hqrs. 11 ORs	A/W.W.M.
	17/10/19		Coy training from 0900 – 1300 1400 – 1500 B.O.C Coys carried out tactical schemes. "B" Range at J.14.c central alloted as follows D Coy 0900 – 1100 A Coy 1100 – 1300 Bradote carried out inoculation 10 ORs. ds. to hospital from Hqrs. 1 OR. 2/Lieut J. CRAWFORD from Hqrs. 1 OR from Base. To Hosp. 6 ORs sick.	Arteries?
	18/10/19		Company training tactical schemes etc from 0900 – 1200 Lecture 1500 – 1700. Box Respirators station gas chamber from 1400 – Coys at half hour interval. Warning orders received that divisions would move EASTWARD on the 19 inst. Join the VIII Corps. From Hqrs 6 ORs. To Hqrs 1 OR (sick)	A/W.W.L.

WAR DIARY
or
INTELLIGENCE SUMMARY.

Army Form C. 2118.

Place	Date	Hour	Summary of Events and Information	Remarks and references to Appendices
LIENCOURT.	19/10/18		Ref. Map. Sheet 51(c) 1:40000. Move orders received. Moved to cups at DIIS. Battalion paraded at 0830 marched via AVENES-LE-COMTE – HABARCQ – to "FRAZER CAMP" MOUNT ST ELOY. Batt. halted for one hour near BOIS DE HABARCQ for midday meal. Arrived at Mount St Eloy about 1600 – after evening meal took inspection near Carried out by platoon. Lt. Myft. Sick 3. ORs	BATTN ORDER Nº 6
MOUNT ST. ELOY.	20/10/18		Ref. Map. LENS II. 1:100000. Move orders received. Moved to BDS at 0800. Battn paraded at 0820 & marched via NEUVILLE – ST-VAAST – WILLERVAL – DROCOURT – to HENIN LIETARD. Batt. halted for one hour near DROCOURT, where midday meal was served. Arrived at HENIN LIETARD about 1530 & after evening meal, Rifle & Foot inspection were carried out. 2 ORs Lt. Myft. Sick. 2/Lieut H.H. REID joined unit for duty.	BATTN ORDER Nº 7

Army Form C. 2118.

WAR DIARY
or
INTELLIGENCE SUMMARY.
(Erase heading not required.)

Place	Date	Hour	Summary of Events and Information	Remarks and references to Appendices
HENIN LIETARD	21/10/18		New orders issued to coys at 0020. Batta paraded at 0915 & marched via main HENIN LIETARD / DOUAI Rd to FLERS arriving about 1200. Afternoon devoted to rifle & foot inspection. It will be arranged that Batth would probably stay in FLERS for a day or two. 2 Offr Sick. 2 ORs killed. W.u.u.N.	BATTN ORDER Nº 8
FLERS	22/10/18		Day devoted to cleaning up & readjusting equipment. Bath under company arrangement from H.Q.H. 3 ORs proceed in	
FLERS	23/10/18		Coy training, tactical schemes in co-operation with section of L.T.M.B., demonstration of smoke grenades & L.G. service etc. Warning order received that Batn would move E. to MONTREVIL on 24th inst. 1 Offr sick 2 ORs, from H.Q.H. 3 ORs	

Army Form C. 2118.

WAR DIARY
or
INTELLIGENCE SUMMARY.
(Erase heading not required.)

Place	Date	Hour	Summary of Events and Information	Remarks and references to Appendices
			Ref Trench Sheet 44ᵃ 1/40000	
FLERS	24/10/18		Battn parade at 0855. Marched via DOUAI – RACHES – MONTREUIL – to FLINES, arriving about 1400. Afternoon devoted to rifle & foot inspection, settling in billets.	BATTN Order No 9. To Hospital sick 1.O.R. WWW
FLINES	25/10/18		Battalion parade at 0830 for road cleaning, repairing – removal of worn A, B, C & D Coys area FLINES village. Two half hours of training area FLINES/MARCHIENNES RD. carried out during the period.	To Hospital sick 1.O.R. WWW. From Hospital 3.O.Rs WWW.
" "	26/10/18		C.O with Lts. RICHARDSON & HENRY left Bde Headquarters at 0830 to reconnoitre the line near ST AMAND. Battn carried out training from 0900–1200 1400–1500 general work. Warning orders received that battalion would proceed to LANDAS on the 27th inst. Capt A ODEAS to Divn Staff – GSO3	To Hospital sick 1.O.R. From Hospital 1.O.R. To Bde HQrs for duty 3.O.R. WWW

WAR DIARY or INTELLIGENCE SUMMARY

Army Form C. 2118.

Ref Map Sheet 44 1:40.000

Place	Date	Hour	Summary of Events and Information	Remarks and references to Appendices
FLINES	27/10/18		Battalion parade at 11.15. Marched via ORCHIES to LANDAS arriving about 14.45. Remainder of day devoted to settling in billets – Rifle + foot inspection.	BATTN ORDER No 10
"	28/10/18		Battn parade at 12.00, marched to LACELLES arriving about 14.45. Remainder of the day devoted to settling in billets. 10 R from hospital 10 R. To hospital 2/Lt G. HADDOCK & 10 R	ORDER No 11
"	29/10/18		Day devoted to cleaning up billets – scrubbing & generally cleaning of equipment + clothing. To hospital sick 10 R. From hospital 10 R.	
"	30/10/18		About 04.30 four 5.9 H.E. shells landed in the vicinity of the transport lines. Killed 10 R. Wounded 4 O R. Battn parade at 09.00 – 12.00 Company training. Battalion parade 15.00 marched to RUE BOUCHIN J.19 arriving about 16.00. A few shells of heavy calibre landed in area throughout the night. To hospital sick 4 OR. From hospital 10 R.	

WAR DIARY or INTELLIGENCE SUMMARY

Army Form C. 2118.

Place	Date	Hour	Summary of Events and Information	Remarks and references to Appendices
Rue Bouchin J.19	31/10/18		Ref Map Sheet 44 1:40000 Company training under company arrangements from 0900-1200. 1400-1500 to hospital sick 3 O.R. from L.T.M.B. 1 O.R. from L.T.M.B. 1 O.R.	

Summary of Casualties Etc. for October - 1918.

Increase

	Offs.	O.Rs.	Total
From Hospital (W)	-	11	11
" " (S.K.)	A 3	17	20
Draft Reinforcements	B 14	19	33
Taken on Strength of Unit	C 1	3	4
Total	**18**	**110**	**128**

Decrease

	Offs.	O.Rs.	Total
To Hospital Sick & Died of Wds	D 1	1	2
" Hosp. (Sick)	E 3	10	13
" " (W)	-	22	22
Struck off Effective Strength	F 2	5	7
Total	**6**	**98**	**104**

'A'
2/Lt. D. Darby 2/7/18
Lt. W. Muir 8/7/18
2/Lt. S. Crayford 14/7/18

'C'
Lt. A.W. Philip (Supplies interior) 4/7/18 (Div. Employ)

'B'
2/Lt. R.H. Canning 1/7/18
" D.H. McLagan 2/7/18
" R. Brown
" McCallum a/t/Lt. J.K. Jordan 5/7/18
2/Lt. R.J. Evans 8/7/18
" 2/Lt. R.J. Inglis 8/7/18
Capt. J. Lloyd Stone 9/7/18
2/Lt. D.P. McLagan 9/7/18
" J. Murray 10/7/18
" J.R. Campbell 14/7/18
2/Lt. A.R. Reid 20/7/18

'D'
2/Lt. S.L. Vallance 29/9/18 att 8 L.T.M.B.

'E'
2/Lt. J. Campbell 3/7/18
" G.B. Ritchie 12/7/18
" J.J. Hadstock 28/7/18

'F'
Major S. Little to 4th R.S.F 5/7/18
Capt R.A.O. DEPN to Div on A.S.O 3. 26/7/18

COPY NO :- 8.

1/7th (Blythswood) Battalion - The Highland Light Infantry.

M O V E   O R D E R S   No. 3.
By Major C. Gibb .... Commanding.,

30th Septbr. 1918.

REFERENCE SHEET :- 57c N.E.

1. The 157th Infantry Brigade will move East tomorrow and take over the Line from the 63rd Division in F.30 and be in support to 155 INF. Bde..

2. 5th H.L.I. will be on the right; 6th H.L.I. on Left and 7th H.L.I. in reserve.

3. (1)   Order of March commencing 1400:-
         6th H.L.I.,
         5th H.L.I.,
         7th H.L.I.,
         157th L.T.M.B.,

Starting Point:- CAMBRAI ROAD CANAL CROSSING E27c 1.3. 500 yds distance will be maintained between Bns. and 100 yds between Coys.

(11). 7th H.L.I., will parade at 1400 Each Coy at its present bivouac in readiness to march on the signal being given; when Coys will move forward and gain their correct order and distances.

    Order of March .... H. Qrs Coy.
                            A. Coy.
                            C. Coy.
                            D. Coy.
                            B. Coy, Lewis Guns and S.A.A.

and Malteses Cart.   wagons.

4. The Commanding Officer and Coy Commanders will meet the B.G.C. at CANAL CROSSING E27 C1.3 mounted and accompanied by grooms at 1100.

5. The I.O. will meet the Bde. I.O., mounted. at CANAL CROSSING E27 c1 3. at 0900 tomorrow to proceed in advance to reconnoitre L'ESCAUT CANAL and RIVER CROSSING, and best route from EAST OF CANTAING.

6. (1) Limbered G.S. Wagons carrying Lewis Guns and S.A.A. also Maltese Cart will accompany Battalions. The remaining Transport, i,e. Field Kitchens, Water Carts, tool carts and Baggage Wagons will march under the orders of the Staff Captain after all Units have passed the STarting Point in same order of march as Units (viz. 6th, 5th, 7th H.L.I.)

(11) Transport of 7th H.L.I., will draw up on Road running through E26d with head of column clear of main CAMBRAI ROAD; ready to move off at 1430.

7. A hot meal in Cookers will be ready for men when transport arrives at the new area.

8. Nucleus will remain at Battalion Transport Lines and not return to Divisional Reception Camp.

9. Rations will be issued on arrival at new Transport Lines.

10. Water Carts will move full. Water has been ordered for 12 noon to enable this to be done.

11. Greatcoats will be carried by the man in the pack. (If leather Jerkins are issued before moving off they will be carried in the pack and not worn.)

12. Tents and Trench Shelters will be dumped at Bn. Hd. Qrs by 1230; the shelters being rolled in bundles of five.

13. Midday meal will be at 1200.

Copy No.   1   Hd. Qrs Coy.
           2   A. Coy.
           3   B. Coy.
           4   C. COY.
           5   D. Coy.
           6   Q. M.
      7&8   War Diary.
           9   Office File.

Lieut. & A/Adjt.,
1/7th Bn H. L. I.

SECRET.   COPY No. 8.

1/7th (Blythswood) Battalion – The Highland Light Infantry.

ORDER No. 5.
By Major J. H. Foster.   Commanding.

7th October 1918.

-:-:-:-:-:-:-:-:-:-:-?-:-:-:-:-:-:-:-

REFERENCE MAP LENS 11.1/10,000. also Sheet 57c N.E. 1 20,000.

1. The 157 Infantry Brigade Group will proceed to-day, 7th October, to the HOUVIN AREA, entraining at VAULX-VRACOURT, and detraining at PETIT-HOUVIN.

2. Order of March :- The following will be the order of march to the entraining station.

157 Brigade	Time to pass starting point
Headquarters	1430
7th H.L.I.	1435.
6th H.L.I.	1500.
157 L.T.M.B.	1545.
5th H.L.I.	1550.

Distances of 500 yards between Battalions and 100 yards between Companies will be maintained on the march. 10 minutes halt will be observed at 10 minutes to every hour.

3. (a) STARTING POINT. - Cross Roads where MOUVRES-DERICOURT Road crosses CAMBRAI-BAPAUME ROAD.
  (b) ROUTE. From present Camp BOURSIES - CROSSROADS M. of Z via BEAUMETZ-LE-CAMBRAI - NORCHIES and VAULX-VRACOURT.
  (c) The Battalion will parade ready to move off at 1400. head of the Column facing SOUTH, at CROSS ROADS.
     Order of march :-
        Battalion Headquarters Coy.
        A. Coy.
        B. Coy.
        C. Coy.
        D. Coy.   Dress :- Full marching order as given out to Coy Cdrs. Water Bottles to be filled.

4. TENTAGE. :- Bivouac Sheets rolled in bundles of 5, will be stacked at Battalion Headquarters at 0630. The Sgt. Major will detail a loading party from headquarters for that hour.

5. Valises will be stacked at Transport Lines by 0900. O.C. A. Coy will detail 1 Officer and 7 men to report to Battn. Hdqrs at 0800. They will proceed with valises.

6. Dinner will be at 1300. All Dixies must be returned immediately after

7. DETRAINING OFFICER. Capt. Boyd will report to the R.T.O. at HOUVIN on the arrival of the train. He will remain on duty until troops have detrained from No. 7 the last train.

8. UNLOADING PARTY. :- O.C. B. Coy will detail an unloading party of 1 Officer and 30 other ranks for duty at the detraining station.

9. Battalion will proceed by No. 7 Train leaving VAULX-VRACOURT at 1915. arriving at PETIT HOUVIN 2300.

10. Mess Stores will be dumped at Batt. Headquarters by 1330.

11. ACKNOWLEDGE.

Copy No. 1 O.C. A. Coy.
         2 O.C. B. Coy.
         3 O.C. C Coy.
         4 O.C. D. Coy.
         5. O.C. Hdqrs Coy.
         6. T.O.
    7 &8. War Diary.
         9 Office File.

Lieut. & A/Adjt.
7th Bn H.L.I.

issued at on 7/10/18 by Runner,

REFERENCE BATTALION ORDER NO. 5 OF 7/10/18.

MARCH DISCIPLINE.

Strict March Discipline will be maintained throughout the march. Troops will march in 4s. One Officer will march in rear of each Company, O.C. D. Coy will detail 1 platoon to act as rear party. They will march 100 yards behind the Company. At each halt men will take off equipment. They must fall out and fall in quickly and quietly.

TRAIN DISCIPLINE.

Strict Discipline will be observed. No man is to enter or leave the train without orders from an Officer. O.C. Coys will detail an N.C.O. to be in charge of each wagon. Entraining and detraining must be carried out in silence.

Lieut. & A/Adjt.
1/7th Bn H. L. I.

SECRET.   Copy No. 11

1/7th (Blythswood) Battalion   The Highland Light Infantry
                                              No. 6.
         M O V E   O R D E R S.
    By Lieut. Col. J. H. Foster, Commanding.   19/10/18.

---

1. 157 Infantry Brigade Group will proceed by route march on the 19th, inst. to the MONT ST. ELOI area.
2. Battalion will parade ready to move off at 0850. Head of column facing East at Liencourt Station.
3. <u>Order of march.</u>   Headquarters, C. B. A. D. L.T.M. Battery, and Transport.   <u>Dress</u> :-   Marching Order, jerkins in packs.   Distance of 500 yards will be observed between Units, and 100 yards between Companies.
4. <u>Route.</u>   AVENES-LE-COMTE - HARBARCQ - Junction of roads S.E. edge BOIS D'HARBARCQ - MONT ST. ELOI.
5. Halt of 1 hour for mid-day meal will be observed approximately from 1300 - 1400.   Mid-day meal must be ready for issue from cookers immediately the Battalion halts.   On no account will the halt be extended.
6. O.C. "C" Coy. will detail a strong platoon under an Officer to stay behind and clean up billeting area.   Officer will then obtain a certificate from the Area Commandant that this has been done.
7. Greatcoats and blankets will be carried on motor transport. They will be rolled in bundles of ten and stacked at Q.M. Stores by 0730.   O.C. "A" Coy. will detail a strong platoon under an Officer to report to Q.M. as loading party at 0730.
8. Officers valises and Mess kit will be stacked at Q.M. Stores immediately-after-reveille at 0730.
9. Lewis Guns and magazines will be taken to Q.M. Stores immediately after reveille.
10. Cookers will follow immediately in rear of their respective Coys.
11. Billets must be left scrupulously clean.
12. All area stores will be handed in to Area Commandant and receipts obtained.
13. Strict march discipline will be observed throughout march. No man will fall out without permission from an Officer.
14. Men warned to proceed on leave to U.K., sailing from BOULOGNE on 21st instant, will parade at O.R. at 0800 prompt ready to proceed.
15. ACKNOWLEDGE.

                                        Lieut. & A/Adjt.,
                                        1/7th Bn. H. L. I.

Copy No. 1   O.C.   A.   Coy.
          2.   B.
          3.   C.
          4.   D.
          5.   H.Q.
          6.   L.T.M.B.
          7.   T.O.
          8.   Q.M.
          9.   R.S.M.
         10.   War Diary.
         11.   War Diary.
         12.   Office.
Issued at : 0115 on 19/10/18
         BY Orderly.

COPY. No.- 8

SECRET.

1/7th. (BLYTHSWOOD) BATTALION - THE HIGHLAND LIGHT INFANTRY.

M O V E   O R D E R. No. 7.
By Lieut-Colonel J.R. Foster.........Commanding.

10th. Octr. 1918.

-:-:-:-:-:-:-:-:-:-:-:-:-:-:-:-:-:-:-:-

REFERENCE MAP - LENS 1: 1/100,000.

1. The Division will continue to move towards BERLIN tomorrow, 20th Inst.
   The 157th Infantry Brigade Group will proceed by Route March to the HENIN LIETARD AREA where it will bivouac for the night.

2. The starting point will be at Brigade Headquarters (at White House). The following will be the order of march:-
                                                   Time to pass starting
                                                   point.
   Brigade Headquarters.............................0520.
   7th. H.L.I. (followed by 157th L.T.M.B.).........0535.
   5th. H.L.I......................................0600.
   6th. H.L.I......................................0615.

   The Battalion will parade on road between huts ready to move off at 0530. Head of the column S.E. end of the present Camp.   Order of March:-
                Headquarters.
                B. Coy.
                A. Coy.
                D. Coy.
                C. Coy.
                Transport.

3. A distance of 300 yards will be maintained between Units, and 100 yards between Companies throughout the march.

4. March discipline must be improved, particularly as regard keeping well to the right of the road. Transport must not be allowed to straggle.

5. ROUTE:- From the starting Point, NEUVILLE-ST-VAAST- THELUS - BAILLEUL-ARLEUX-EN-GOHELLE-DROCOURT-HENIN LIETARD.

6. A halt of 1 hour for midday meal will take place about 1030.

7. O.C. "B" Coy. will detail 1 strong platoon and 1 Officer as a rear party, to stay behind and clean up Billets. The Officer will obtain certificate from the Area Commandant or his representative that the Billets have been left clean. This party will report to the QuarterMaster at 0700.

8.   REVEILLE................0330.
           BREAKFAST...............0415.

9. Blankets and Greatcoats will be rolled in bundles of 10, and securely tied and labled, and stacked at the end of Coy. Huts nearest to road by 0545.

10. Officers valises and Mess Stores must be stacked at Q.M. Stores at 0545.

11. Cookers will march in rear of their respective Companies.

12. ADVANCE PARTY:- An advance party of 1 Junior N.C.O. per Coy. will report with bicycles at Orderly Room at 0500. 2/Lt. Bruce will take charge of this party, and will report to the STAFF CAPTAIN at Brigade Headquarters at 0530.

P.T.O

2.

13. ACKNOWLEDGE.

                                                    [signature]
                                            LIEUT. & A/ADJT.,
                                            1/7th. Bn. H.L.I.,

No. 1 Copy............O.C. "A" Coy.
    2   "   ....   "   "B" "
    3   "   ....   "   "C" "
    4   "   ....   "   "D" "
    5   "   ....   H.Q.
    6   "   ....   Q.M. & T.O.
    7   "   ....   War Diary.
    8   "   ....   War Diary.
    9   "   ....   Office File.

Issued by Adjt
Cat 0360

SECRET.   Copy No. 10

1/7th. (Blythswood) Battalion   The Highland Light Infantry.
B A T T A L I O N   O R D E R S.   No. 8.

By Lieut. Col. E. H. Foster, Commanding.   22/10/18

---

1. The 52nd. Division will continue to march Eastwards to-morrow.

2. The 157 Infantry Brigade Group will proceed by route march to FLERAS PLANQUE and WAHOWVILLE. Starting point will be at C.W.b.7.4. Following will be order of march :— Bde. Hqrs. 5th. H.L.I., 6th. H.L.I., 7th. H.L.I.

3. Battalion will parade ready to march off about 0815 ; exact hour to be notified later. Distances of 300 yards between Units and 100 yards between Coys. will be maintained. Order of march : Hqrs., A., B., C., D. Head of Column at Bn. Hqrs. facing East.

4. Route. MAIN MENIN-LIETARD DOUAI ROAD.

5. Advance party of 1 Junior N.C.O. per Coy. will report with bicycles under 2/Lieut. BRUCE at Orderly Room at 0705.

6. O.C. A Coy. will detail strong platoon under an officer as rear party to clear up. They will report to Quartermaster at Stores at 0720.

7. Blankets and greatcoats will be rolled in bundles of ten (securely tied and labelled) and officers valises will be stacked in the last house (facing level crossing) at the West end of A. Coys. billets. Mess stores will be dumped at same place at 0630.

8. Reveille will be at 0540 ; breakfast at 0700.

9. ACKNOWLEDGE.

                                                        Lieut. & A/Adjt.,
                                                        1/7th. Bn. H.L.I.

Distribution.
Copy No. 1.   O.C. A. Coy.
        2.   B.
        3.   C.
        4.   D.
        5.   H.Q.
        6.   Q.M.
        7.   T.O.
        8.   R.S.M.
        9.   War Diary.
       10.   Office.

Issued by Orderly at :—

SECRET.   Copy NO. 10

1/7th. (-lythswood) Battalion   The Highland Light Infantry.

BATTALION ORDERS. No, 9.

By Lieut. Col. J. H Foster, Commanding.   23/10/18.

Ref. MAP SHEET 44 A. 1/40, 999.

1. The 157 Infantry Brigade will move to the MONTREUIL Area to-morrow, the 24th, instant.

2. The Battalion will parade ready to move off at 0855 : head of the column at Battalion Headquarters Mess facing South, Order of march :- Hqrs, D. A. B. C. Transport. Dress :- marching order. Distance of 500 yards between Units and 100 yards between Coys, will be maintained.

3. Route :-   DOUAI : RACHES : PT. BAILON : MONTREUIL.

4. Reveille will be at 0600. Breakfast at 0630,

5. Blankets and greatcoats will be rolled in bundles of 10. securely tied and labelled, and stacked at Q.M. Stores at 0700.   Officers valises at 0730!

6. Officers' Mess Stores will be dumped at Q.M. Stores at 0800.

7. Field Cookers and Lewis Gun Limbers will follow immediately in rear of their respective Coys.

8. O.C. B. Coy. will detail a strong platoon under an Officer as rear party to clear up.   Party will report to Quartermaster at 0700,

9. The guard will march in rear of the battalion under the Orderly Officer, and will pick up and bring on any stragglers

10. Attention of Coy. Commanders is drawn to recent march discipline orders.

11. Billets must be left as clean as possible.

12. ACKNOWLEDGE.

                                                Lieut& A/Adjt.,
                                                1/7th, Bn. H. L. I.

Distribution.
Copy No. 1.   O.C.ACoy.
          2.   B.
          3.   C.
          4.   D.
          5.   H.Q.
          6.   T.O.
          7.   Q.M.
          8.   R.S.M.
          9.   War Diary.
         10.   -do-
         11.   Office.

Issued by orderly : at 2030.

SECRET.   Copy No. 10

1/7th (Blythswood) Battalion   The Highland Light Infantry

BATTALION ORDERS   No. 10.

By Lieut. Col. J.H. Foster, Commanding.   26/10/18

Reference Map Sheet 44, 1/40,000

1. 157 Infantry Brigade will move by march route to Landas to-morrow, the 27th instant.

2. Battalion will parade ready to move off at 1030 : head of column facing North. Head of column at Bn. Hqr. Mess.
Order of march :- A. B. C. and D. Coys.
Distance of 500 yards to be maintained between Units and 100 yards between Coys.
Dress :- Marching Order, greatcoats in packs, jerkins neatly rolled and strapped on top of packs.

3.   Reveille .... 0630.
             Breakfast .... 0800.

4. Rear Party.   O.C. C. Coy will detail a strong platoon under an Officer as rear party to clean up.   This party will report to Quarter-master at 0700.   Certificate will be obtained by the Officer before leaving that billets have been left in a clean and sanitary condition.

5. BLANKETS.   Blankets will be rolled in bundles of 10 securely tied and labelled, and stacked at Quarter-master Stores, at 0700. Officers valises and Mess Stores at 0800.

6. Field Kitchens and Lewis Gun Limbers will follow behind their respective Coys.

7. Guard will march at the rear of the battalion under the Orderly Officer, and will pick up and bring on any stragglers.

8. ACKNOWLEDGE.

                                                    Lieut. & A/Adjt.
                                                    1/7th Bn. H.L.I.

Distribution.
Copy No. 1   O.C. A. Coy.
          2   B.
          3   C.
          4   D.
          5   H.Qs.
          6   T.O.
          7   Q.M.
          8   R.S.M.
          9   War Diary
         10   DO.
         11   Office.

Issued by Orderly at 2140.

SECRET. Copy No. 10

1/7th (Blythswood) Battalion The Highland Light Infantry.

B A T T A L I O N   O R D E R S   NO. 11.

By Lieut. Col. J.H. Foster, Commanding. 27/10/18.

Ref. Map Sheet 44. 1/40,000.

1. The 152 Infantry Brigade Group will march to LACELLES to-morrow, the 27th. instant.

2. Battalion will parade ready to move off at 1200 : head of column at Q.M. Stores facing S.E. Order of march :- Hqrs., B.C.D.A. DRESS :- Marching Order, as for to-day. Distance of 500 yards to be maintained between Units and 100 yards between Coys.

3. Reveille will be at 0700 : Breakfast at 0800. Sick Parade at 0820. Mid-day Meal at 1100.

4. Officers valises will be stacked at Q.M. Stores at 1000 : Mess Stores at 1130.

5. REAR PARTY. O.C. D. Coy. will detail a strong platoon under an Officer as rear party. This party will report to Q.M. at 1000. The Officer will obtain a certificate from Town Major that billets have been left in a clean and sanitary condition.

6. ADVANCE PARTY of 1 N.C.O. per Coy., Headquarters and Transport, under 2/Lieut. Bruce, will parade with bicycles and report at Orderly Room at 0830.

7. Platoon Commanders will personally supervise packing of packs.

8. Commanding Officer's Orderly Room will be at 1000 to-morrow.

9. O.C., Coys. are reminded that when men are given permission to fall out they must be instructed to report to the Medical Officer in rear of Battalion.

10. The Guard will march at the rear of the battalion under the Orderly Officer and will pick up and bring on any stragglers.

11. ACKNOWLEDGE.

Lieut. & A/Adjt.,
1/7th Bn H.L.I.

Distribution.
Copy No. 1. O.C. A. Coy.
2. B.
3. C.
4. D.
5. H.Qrs.
6. T.O.
7. Q.M.
8. R.S.M.
9. War Diary.
10. do.
11. Office.

By orderly at 1110.

1/7th BATTALION, HIGHLAND LIGHT INFANTRY.
No. 21/18

7th Batt. H. L. I.

Vol 8

War Diary for November 1915

9.F
13 sheets

Army Form C. 2118.

WAR DIARY
or
INTELLIGENCE SUMMARY.
(Erase heading not required.)

Place	Date	Hour	Summary of Events and Information	Remarks and references to Appendices
La Bouchein J.19	1/8		Ref Map Sheet 44 1:40,000 Training continued under Coy arrangements 0730-1200 & 1400-1800 – Usual scheme of general training from hospital 80R. 2 hospl.	
"	2/8		12 OR (not gas) 10R sick. Battalion tactical scheme by platoon – afternoon devoted to cleaning & scrubbing equipment. To hospital 10R sick. 1 OR wd gas. 1 OR wd gas.	
"	3/8		Scheme resumed at 0930. Warning mid received that Battn would take over the line on the 4th inst. Capt A.D. Seiu taken on the strength – Capt W Leonard reports for duty. 1 O.R. wd. 7 H. Draft of 1 O.R. joined.	
"	4/8		C.O. & Coy Commanders left at 0800 to reconnoitre the line. Battalion turned out at 1300 & marched-would via ST AMAND-LA CROISETTE – took over the line from 2nd WEST YORKS NW of FRESNES. relief completed at 2015. Platoons under Major Watson remained with transport at LA CROISETTE.	ORDER No. 12
near FRESNES	5/8		Artillery quiet – MGs & T MORTARS fairly active. Small patrol worked along the FRESNES/RONDE STN RD but owing to broken glass quiet going was impossible patrol returned from Hostile. 2nd Lt A.J. Petrie to hospl. 2 OR sick. 2OR wd gas. Hostile sh wd. ft.	

WAR DIARY or INTELLIGENCE SUMMARY

Army Form C. 2118.

Place	Date	Hour	Summary of Events and Information	Remarks and references to Appendices
West FRESNES	6/9		Ref. Trench Sheet 44.d 1:40,000. Normal. Patrol 1 Officer & 1 Rifle section proceeded along Fresnes/Condé Stn Rd about 20x when enemy was heard in vicinity. Patrol took up a defensive position & returned having seen no enemy. Patrol moved on NEO left Q.4 c & 8 & proceeded along track to north at K.34 d 4.1 & found bridge destroyed. M.G. Hammering fire from enemy during the night. From Hospl. 4 O.R. To Hospl. 5 O.R. 1 accidt & injured 4 O.R.	
" "	7/9		Normal - Usual enemy fire. 2 patrols were sent forward during the night unhindered having seen no enemy formations. Enemy reported decreasing on the left sector. Coy of 5th HLI relieved A Coy of 1/4 HLI. A Coy withdrawing to Q.17 c 90.15. From Hospl. 3 O.R. To Hospl. 10 R killed 2 O.R. wounded 2 O.R.	Ref. order No 14
" "	8/9		All enemy artillery fire ceased at 0100 but the M.Gs & T.Ms were active about 0630 all field fire ceased, & everything pointed to a withdrawal. A patrol of "O" Coy went down to the river, advanced towards the Canal without drawing fire. Report was sent to Brigade HQrs, & Coy moved "Hunt", which was to commence operations, was moved at 0800. O'clock & the road forward & footbridge in hedges were then thrown across the river. The Canal was then crossed & all footbridges were completed by 1400 - the 6th HLI then went through going East. The battalion was formed - independently by coys - & worked for the night in VIEUX CONDÉ. From Hospl 2 O.R. Draft joined 10 R. To Hospl 2/Lt A.M.BRUCE Ap. NMW/Lt	ORDER NO 13

WAR DIARY or INTELLIGENCE SUMMARY

Army Form C. 2118.

Place	Date	Hour	Summary of Events and Information	Remarks and references to Appendices
VIEUX CONDE	9/11/18		Ref. Map Sheet 44 1:40,000 Battalion paraded at 0530 marched - went to ROSETTE in expectation of 6th HLI arriving about 0830. Orders were issued but further orders were received to move forward. Battalion paraded at 1380 marched went to HARCHIES - luncheon under Major Watson & transport joined Battalion at Te Calvaire - a halt was ordered pending instructions. Battalion afterwards proceeded to POMMEROEUIL & billeted for the night. 'A' Coy who were on outpost duty East of the village. Weather fine.	
POMMEROEUIL	10/11/18		Ref. Map Sheet 45 1:40,000 Battalion paraded less 'B' Coy at 0700 - mechanical transport left to follow on later - marched route via HAUTRAGE to TERTRE thence to BAUDOUR. 'A' Coy then pushed along the BAUDOUR/GHLIN Rd with 'D' Coy in support. 'C' Coy pushing along the DOUVRAIN/GHLIN Rd the situation being its also the ground of enemy & from Rd. GHLIN. Heavy enemy fire was experienced at East side of BAUDOUR. 'A' Coy got in touch with enemy M.Gun at the N outskirts of GHLIN & were held up. 'C' Coy went like wise. Outpost positions was taken up by D & C Coys with A of 'B' Coy - who had joined later by the time - in support later. H Qrs at 1240 'D' luncheon & transport billeted in BAUDOUR. Yo Hospl 3 OR Sick 3 OR wounded. Weather Lt.	

WAR DIARY
or
INTELLIGENCE SUMMARY.

(Erase heading not required.)

Army Form C. 2118.

Place	Date	Hour	Summary of Events and Information	Remarks and references to Appendices
Near GHLIN	11/8/14		Ref. Map Sheet 45. 1:40,000. Everyone woke next great expectations the fronts was exceedingly quiet. About 0900 a mounted officer from 1 batt. H.Qrs stated that hostilities were to cease at 1100. This was confirmed by mounted orderly from Brigade H.Qrs — message states "hostilities would not begin until 1100 old troops the *kind* part the runner stated". Battalion was relieved by 2nd Middlesex Regt. at 1530 & marched out — nucleus under Major Walton & transport joining at BAUDOUR to VACRESSE arriving about 1900. Y/R S.M. Davis placed for duty.	
VACRESSE	12/8/14		Day devoted to rest rebaning up. From Hopkins 5 OR British.	
"	13/8/14		Cleaning equipment & issuing clothing etc. From Hopkins 1 OR wound L.	
"	14/8/14		Commanding officers inspection of company's. Training commenced. Ceremonial drill & general awakening exercises between it. From Hosptl 4 OR. To Hosptl 2 OR sick.	
"	15/8/14		Battalion moved to MAISIÈRES by march route VIA BRUGOTTE & PAVÉ. Relieved 2nd Middlesex Regt. A & B Coys holding outpost line E of the village. Stand off the strength account over 21 days. To Hosptl 9 OR sick. From Hosptl 3 OR. 2 OR.	Ret + ORDER No 17

Army Form C. 2118.

WAR DIARY
or
INTELLIGENCE SUMMARY.

(Erase heading not required.)

Instructions regarding War Diaries and Intelligence Summaries are contained in F. S. Regs., Part II. and the Staff Manual respectively. Title pages will be prepared in manuscript.

Place	Date	Hour	Summary of Events and Information	Remarks and references to Appendices
MAISIERES	16/11/18		REF MAP. Sheet 45. 1/40000. Battalion training under coy arrangements 0900 - 1000. Handling of arms, guard drill & general training.	
"	17/11/18		Divine service 1000. 2nd Army both over responsibility of front "A" & "B" Coys relieved from outpost duty. From Hosp. 1 OR. To Hosp. 1 OR. Woven L. From Hosp. 3 OR	
"	18/11/18		Training continued. NCOs under R.S.M Davis taken on the along ex 281-284 Sgt. W McCracker G "A" Coy 280 345 " Farris W " 18499 Pte R Blackwood " To Hosp. from Bn. H.Q. 10R. 280900 - A Reilly " 1330 - 1430. "B" Coy moved at 280504 Pte M Laughlin from Bn. To Home service. Authy. CR No 28267/M42/522 "A" To Base changed. Authy BM 18/11/18 Woven L.	
"	19/11/18		Training continued. Parades from 0900 - 1230. Educational classes Woven Commenced tour from 1130 - 1230	
"	20/11/18		Training continued. Ceremonial drill with a view to B.G.C. inspection Woven To	
"	20/11/18		Training continued. Ceremonial drill. Baths allotted to battalion at GHLIN from 1130 - 1430. From Hospital 3 OR. Draft 10R Woven to	
"	22/11/18		Training continued. Ceremonial drill. - From hospital 1 OR. To Hospital 4 OR. Struck off the strength about % UK leave over 21 days 2 OR Woven L.	Yu.

WAR DIARY
INTELLIGENCE SUMMARY

Army Form C. 2118.

Place	Date	Hour	Summary of Events and Information	Remarks and references to Appendices
MAISIERES	23/11/18	Ref Map Sheet 45. 1:40000	Bde ceremonial parade at 1000. Inoculation parade in the afternoon from hospital 1.O.R. to hospital 2.O.R. [2nd Lieut admitted to Wei Lt to hospital 1.O.R. returned from leave]	
"	24/11/18		Commanding officers inspection of billets at 1400. Divine service at 1100. from hospital 2/Lt A.M.C.K. Bruce & G Haddock 1.O.R. Draft 2.O.R. Wei Lt	
"	25/11/18		Parades including arrangements, running &c.ran carried out in billets Bde Lewis Gun school commenced. Commanding officers lecture on 'Demobilization' 1430. from hospital 5.O.R. to hospital 1.O.R. to tour of duty at Home 3.O.R.	Wei Lt
"	26/11/18		"A" coy on range at K14 & 43. B.C. & D. coys carried out Tactical schemes. from hospital 1.O.R.	Wei Lt
"	27/11/18		Training under company arrangements. officers on demob. to spend from hospital 1.O.R. to hospital 1.O.R. (returning from leave)	Wei Lt
"	28/11/18		Battalion ceremonial parade. Lt. Col. Foster proceeded to England for course at CAMBERLEY Major WATSON M.C. assumed command of the battalion. from hospital 5.O.R.	Wei Lt

Army Form C. 2118.

WAR DIARY
or
INTELLIGENCE SUMMARY.
(Erase heading not required.)

Place	Date	Hour	Summary of Events and Information	Remarks and references to Appendices
MAISIERES	29/11		Trench Rft Sheet 45. 1/40,000. Training carried out under company arrangements. "B" Coy on Rifle range 0900 – 1320 – Educational classes continued. From hospital 2 O.R. to hospital 2 O.R. Major L.D. Murray struck off the strength of Unit Authy – E. Q. G. No 13/495 (M) to Wei Zk No Wei Zk.	
"	30/11		Training continued 0900 – 1100. "B" Coy supplies working party at range. Period 0830 – 1100. B.Q.C.'s lecture to Officer & Colour Sergts. 1130. Afternoon devoted to sports. To hospital 3 O.R.	

Summary of Casualties for November 1918.

		Offrs	O.R.	Total
Increase.	From Hospital (Accdn) A	1	32	33
	" (S.K.) B	2	35	37
	Draft Reinforcements C	1	27	28
	Return on Strength of Unit. D	1	6	7
	Total.	5	100	105

		Offrs	O.R.	Total
Decrease.	Killed in action.	—	2	2
	To Hospital (Accdn)	—	16	16
	" (S.K.) E	1	40	41
	Struck off Strength of Unit. F	1	18	19
	Total.	2	76	78

A 2/Lt A.J. Patrie. 5/11
B 2/Lt G. Addcock } 24/11
  " A.M. Bruce.
C Capt N.S. Lennart. 3/11
D Capt A.D. Dun. 3/11
E 2/Lt A.M. Bruce. 8/11
F Major L.D. Murray 29/11.

SECRET.   Copy No. 9

   1/7th. (Blythswood) Battalion   The Highland Light Infantry.

                    O R D E R   N O.   18. 12
            By Lieut. Col. J. H. Foster, Commanding.   4/11/18

---

1. 157 Infantry Brigade will relieve the 23rd. Infantry Brigade, 7th. H.L.I. taking over from 2nd. West Yorks., in the front line.

2. The Battalion will parade ready to move off at 1300, head of the column at Headquarters Mess facing East.
   Order of march :-   Headquarters, A. B. C. D. Coys and Transport Nucleus will parade with their Coys.

3. Usual distances will be maintained between Coys. through-out the march.

4. Coys. will be clear of billets by 1200.   Billets to be left clean inside and out.

5. Mid-day meal at 1130.

6. Transport will be loaded at 1230 ; valises and surplus kit stores stacked at Q.M. Stores at that time.

                                          Owen
                                      Lieut. & A/Adjt.,
                                      1/7th. Bn. H.L.I.

4/11/18.

Distribution.
Copy No. 1.   O.C. A. Coy.
         2.   B.
         3.   C.
         4.   D.
         5.   HQs.
         6.   T.O.
         7.   Q.M.
         8.   R.S.M.
     9 and 10.   War Diary.
        11.   Office.

              Ref. More Order No. 18:

   Coys. will relieve Coys. of 2nd. West Yorks as follows :-
A. Coy. 7th. H.L.I. will relieve A. Coy. 2nd. West Yorks.
B.   do.   B.   do.
C.   do.   D.   do.
D.   do.   C.   do.
        1 guide per Coy. and Hqrs. will meet Bn. at Q.12.c.6.9.

   Lewis Guns.   One limber will be allotted to each Coy. for Lewis Guns and surplus stores.   These will go with Coys. to respective areas
           Battalion Hqrs. will be at Q.2.d.9.9.
   Nucleus party will parade at O.Room under Major Watson at 1245.

   Completion of relief will be sent by runner to Bn. Hqrs. using code work "DEAD".   Attention must be paid to sending this immediately relief is complete.

                                          Owen
                                      Lieut. & A/Adjt.,
                                       1/7th. H.L.I.

4/11/18.

SECRET.   Copy No.

/7th. (Blythswood) Battalion   The Highland Light Infantry.
                O R D E R   N O. 13.
        By Lieut. Col. J. H. Foster, Commanding.   7/11/18.
        ───

                Reference Map :   Sheet No. 44 N.E. and S.E. 1/20,000.

1.   When the enemy withdraws the 2nd. Division will follow him up
and keep in touch with his main force.   It is not the
intention that Battalions should become heavily engaged.

2.   As soon as the enemy's withdrawal from the YARD Canal is
ascertained the following will be the procedure :- river and
        (i)   Single file bridges will be thrown across the canal as under :
                (Q.5.c.95.85.   to be known as "G" Bridge.
                (Q.5.b.7.7.   to be known as "K" Bridge.

                (K.34.d.5.1.   to be known as "L" Bridge.
        Covering (K.34.d.7.7.   to be known as "M" Bridge
        Carrying parties for each of the above pairs of bridges
(G. and K. - L. and M.) will be found from the left
Coy. of the front line Battalion, two platoons to each pair.
These platoons will ferry across the river in the rafts and
make good the ground between the river and the canal.
Similarly on arrival of the rafts for the canal bridges
these two platoons will ferry across the canal, and make
good a bridge head along the line -   K.34.b.central, E
K.36.a.95.70. along road running South-east through RIUX
de CONDE to about K.36.c.central,   about Q.6.b.0.6. canal.
                Two sections "D" Coy., M.G. Coy. will accompany
left Company of the front line Battalion, 1 pair of guns to
each bridge

        (ii) Centre Company of front line Battalion will be responsible
for watching the ground between the river and the canal, in
Q.6.c. and d., from position along Southern bank of the
river.   This Company will also take one anti-aircraft
Lewis Gun, mounted.   have

        (iii) Carrying parties for the material for above bridges will
be found as follows :
For G and K Bridges by reserve Company of front line Battn.
For L and M Bridges by one Company of reserve Battalion,
the latter Company being billeted in Q.9.b.
The above Companies will provide not less than 40 carriers each
        On completion of work the carrying parties will return to
their billets, and "stand-by".   Anti-aircraft Lewis
Guns will be placed in vicinity of bridges by Companies
furnishing carrying parties.

        (iv) Bridging operations will be supervised by an officer and
a section to be detailed by O.C., 415th. Coy. R.E.

        (v)   When the bridges are completed the support Battalion will
push over one Company through the Company of the front line
Battalion.

        As soon as the bridge head is taken over by the support
Battalion the left front line Company of Battalion in the line
will block Western and Northern exits from VIUX - CONDE,
reconnoitring VIUX - CONDE and report as to its occupation or
otherwise by hostile troops.

        The code-word " HUNT" will bring the above orders into
operation without further orders.

        Carrying parties will not wear equipment, but will have
bandolier and rifle.

(2)

6. Battalion Headquarters will remain at its present location.
7. ACKNOWLEDGE.

                                                  Lieut. & A/Adjt.,
                                     1/7th. Bn. H. L. I.

Distribution.

        Issued at :   on 7/11/18 by orderly.

SECRET. COPY NO. 6

1/7th. (Blythswood) Battalion   The Highland Light Infantry.

O R D E R   NO. 14.

By Lieut. Col. J. H. Foster, Commanding.   7/11/18

___

1. 5th. Bn. H.L.I. will take over front line with two Companies to-night, 7th./8th. November, 1918, as follows :-
One Coy. to take over dispositions of "A" Coy., 7th. H.L.I.
One Coy. to take over dispositions of left Company of the Left Battalion of 8th. Canadian Infantry Brigade.
All details of the relief to be arranged between Company Commanders concerned.

2. On completion of relief "A" Coy., 7th. H.L.I. will move to billets in LE TRIEUX DE FRESNES, about Q.18.c.5.2. O.C. "A" Coy. to chose suitable location, and notify Battalion Headquarters.

3. Guide will be sent to Battalion Headquarters by 1700 to guide ration limbers to new location.

Lieut. & A/Adjt.,
1/7th. Bn. H.L.I.

Distribution.

Copy No. 1.   O.C. A. Coy.
         2.   B.
         3.   C.
         4.   D.
         5.   H.Qs.
         6.   War Diary.
         7.   War Diary.
         8.   Office

SECRET.   COPY NO. 8

1/7th. (Blythswood) Battalion - The Highland Light Infantry.

B A T T A L I O N - O R D E R. No. 17.

By Lieut-Colonel J.H. Foster.............Commanding.

14th November, 1918.

---

1. The 7th Bn. H.L.I. will relieve the 2nd Middlesex Regt. in the Southern Section of the VIII Corps Front, tomorrow, 15th inst.,

2. **ORDER OF RELIEF.**
   7th Bn. H.L.I. and 2nd Middlesex.
   "A" Coy. 7th H.L.I. will relieve "A" Coy. 2nd Middlesex.
                       Coy. Headquarters K.16c1.9.
   "B" do.   do.   Will relieve "C" Coy. 2nd Middlesex.
                       Coy. Headquarters K. 2.c5.8.
   "C" do.   do.   will relieve "B" Coy. 2nd Middlesex.
   "D" do.   do.   do.   do.   "D" do.   do.
   Companies will take over Outpost Line as follows:-
        "A" Coy. Right.   "B" Coy. Left.
        "C" & "D" Coys. in reserve in Maisieres.

3. **MOVE OFF.**
   The Battalion will parade ready to march off at 0830. Head of the column at Transport Lines, facing S.E.

4. **ORDER OF MARCH:-**
        Headquarters. A. C. D. & B.

4. **ROUTE.**
   NEULOTT, PAVE, K.19D. MAISIERES.
   B. Coy. will leave the Battalion at Pave and march independently to Coy. Headquarters at K.2c3.8;

5. **ADVANCE PARTIES.**
   All Companies will supply an advance party as follows:-
   1 Officer per Company and 1 N.C.O. per Platoon. 1 N.C.O. from Transport. They will parade at the Orderly Room at 0730. Lieut. McCormick will take charge of the party.

6. **VALISES AC.**
   Officers' Valises and Mess Stores will be dumped at Q.M.Stores at 0730.

7. **REAR PARTY.**
   O.C. C. Coy. will detail a strong platoon under an Officer to parade report at Q.M. Stores at 0730 as loading party. They will afterwards clean up the area.

8. **DRESS.**
   Marching Order, Steel Helmet and Jerkin on packs.

9. **RELIEF.**
   On relief, Companies will send a runner to Battalion Headquarters in Maisieres

10. **SKETCH MAP AC.**
    O.C. A. & B. Coy. will send to Battalion Headquarters sketch map of Disposition with map refrence of outpost and sentry groups as soon as possible after relief.

11.   Reveille........0530.
           Breakfast.......0630.

12. Party for MONS tomorrow is hereby cancelled.
    Civilians are allowed past
13. /The Outpost Line from E. to W. They are to be directed to Chateau at J.8b5.8. No one is allowed to cross the Outpost Line/

                                                      P.T.O./-

2.

13. (Ctd).
Line going from W. to E.

14. ACKNOWLEDGE.

					W Weir
					LIEUT. & ACT/ADJT.,
					1/7th Bn. H.L.I.,

Copy No.
	No.1. O.C. A. Coy.
	   2. B.
	   3. C.
	   4. D.
	   5. M.G.,
	   6. Q.M.,
	   7. O.M.
	   8 & 9. War Diary.
	   10. Office.

ISSUED BY ORDERLY
		AT:- 2245

-:-:-:-:-:-:-:-:-:-:-:-:-

WAR DIARY
or
INTELLIGENCE SUMMARY.
(Erase heading not required.)

Army Form C. 2118.

Place	Date	Hour	Summary of Events and Information	Remarks and references to Appendices
MAISIERES	1/12/15		Ref. Map. Sheet 45 1/40,000 Divine service held in the village hall at 11.30. Commanding officer conference subjects - Billets improvements & training. Reinforcements from U.K. 54 O.R. from Hosp. 2 O.R.	
— " —	2/12/15		'A' Coy proceeded to 28th Battery R.F.A. from artillery demonstration. Battn at GHLIN allotted to the movement of the Institution from 0930 – 1430. Reinforcements from U.K. 31 O.R. To Hosp. 2 O.R. 10 W.O.	
— " —	3/12/15		'B' Coy proceeded to artillery demonstration. 'D' Coy allotted the range at K14 & 3. 'A' & C Coys carried out training near their own arrangements. from Hosp. 1 O.R. 10 W.	
— " —	4/12/15		A party of officers under Lt KENNEDY proceeded to artillery demonstration. D + A Coy supplied work parties for Rifle Range at K8 a 2.0. 'C' Coy allotted range at K14 & 4.3. Battalion was above carried out training under Coy arrangements. Reinforcements from U.K. 26 O.R. from Hosp. 3 O.R. Relieves from Hosp. Weapon (Transport) 5 O.R. To hospital 4 O.R.	
— " —	5/12/15		'D' Coy proceeded to artillery demonstration. Range at K14 & 3 allotted to 'C' Coy. A & B Coys carried out training under Coy arrangements. Reinforcements from U.K. 3 O.R. from Hosp. 2 O.R. To Hosp. 20 R. data	

Army Form C. 2118.

WAR DIARY
or
INTELLIGENCE SUMMARY.
(Erase heading not required.)

Instructions regarding War Diaries and Intelligence Summaries are contained in F.S. Regs., Part II. and the Staff Manual respectively. Title pages will be prepared in manuscript.

Place	Date	Hour	Summary of Events and Information	Remarks and references to Appendices
MAISIERES	6/12/18		Ref. Map Sheet 45c 1/40000. "C" Coy proceeded to artillery demonstration. Remaining Coy's carried out training under Coy arrangements. Junior NCO's parade under the R.S.M. Detach of strength (to have breast) 2.OR. Reinforcements 7 OR. From hospl. 1.OR. to hospl. 2.OR.	W.W.
"	7/12/18		Adjutants parade from 0900 - 0930. Commanding officers parade at 1000 - ceremonial drill. From hospl. 10R. to hospl. 4 OR.	W.W.
"	8/12/18		Divine service. C. of E. parade in Village hall at 1200. Lewis Gun personnel: "A" Coy. Sergts. class under Capt Dunlop. R.T. Lemon divine service to Nile inspections. From hospl. 1 OR.	W.W.
"	9/12/18		Training carried out under Coy arrangements. Lewis Gun personnel. Lewis Gun practice under L.G. officer on Range practice at K.14 & 43. Sergts. class under R.S.M. Reinforcements 3. OR. From hospl. 4 OR.	W.W.
"	10/12/18		Training carried out under Coy arrangement. Lewis Gun personnel of "B" Coy under L.G. officer on Range practice at K.14 & 43. Sergts. class under R.S.M. From hospl. 2.OR.	W.W.

WAR DIARY
or
INTELLIGENCE SUMMARY.
(Erase heading not required.)

Army Form C. 2118.

Place	Date	Hour	Summary of Events and Information	Remarks and references to Appendices
MAISIÈRES	11/12/18		Ref. Map Sheet 45" 1/40,000 Provisional Artillery. Battalion demonstrate infantry training to Single class paraded under the R.S.M. from hopt. 3 OR to hopt. 2 OR M.W.	
"	12/12/18		Training carried out under coy arrangements. Sing. class paraded under the R.S.M. from hopt. 2 OR to hopt. 2 OR M.W.	
"	13/12/18		Training carried out under coy arrangements. Sing. class paraded under the R.S.M. from hopt. 1 OR to hopt. 5 OR M.W.	
"	14/12/18		General Baths at GHLIN allotted to the battalion from 0900-1430. from hopt. 2 OR to hopt. 2 OR M.W.	
"	15/12/18		Divine service held in the village hall at 0930. Commanding officer inspected billets at 1100. from hopt. 6 OR Reinforcements from Base 3 OR OR leave absentee struck off strength 1 OR to hopt. 10 OR M.W.	

Army Form C. 2118.

WAR DIARY
or
INTELLIGENCE SUMMARY.
(Erase heading not required.)

Place	Date	Hour	Summary of Events and Information	Remarks and references to Appendices
MAISIÈRES	16/12/18		Ref. Map. Mal. 40'. 1/40,000. The G.O.C. 32nd Divn. inspected the battalion. Coys were inspected as follows: "A" Coy Close order drill. "B" Coy Rapid moving & taking a strong point. "C" Coy Intentive training. D Coy Tactical Scheme. Training to hoppl. 1.0.R.	
" "	17/12/18		Battalion carried out training under Coy arrangements. Battalion relief of Mons Guard. inspected battalion billets. B.G.C. 15'y Bde. From hopl. 2.0.R.	
" "	18/12/18		Reveille Parade at 0900 till 0930, from 0930 training carried out under Coy arrangements. Sgts Class under the R.S.M. Transferred to 9th Hr.l off Strength L.O.R. to 6th Hr.l do. 10.R. hopl. 10.R. do. From hopl. 2.0.R.	
" "	19/12/18		Owing to rain Coys carried on in billets, also Sergts Class under R.S.M. To hopl. 10.R. From hopl. 2.0.R.	

WAR DIARY or INTELLIGENCE SUMMARY

Army Form C. 2118.

Ref. Map Sheet 45 1:40000

Place	Date	Hour	Summary of Events and Information	Remarks and references to Appendices
MAISIERES	20/12/18		Owing to Rain training carried out in billets under of arrangements from Lonpl. 2OR. Lecture on attempt from Bde Hqrs 2OR to Lonpl. HOR 2os	
"	21/12/18		Adjutants parade 0900 - 0930. Commanding Officers parade commenced until 1000 hours. from hospl 3OR. To hospl. 1OR. 2os	
"	22/12/18		Divine service in Village Hall 0930. - R.C. parade 1030 - Coy E 1800. Commanding Officers conference subject "Improvement of Arms" 1130. from hospl 9OR. To hospl. ?OR. 2os	
"	23/12/18		Battalion baths allotted to 'A' Coy. Range at K8a P2 allotted to 'B' Coy. 'C' & 'D' Coys training under own arrangements. Riding school for officers at 1400. To hospl. 1OR	
"	24/12/18		Baths allotted to 'B' Coy. Range at K8 a.6.2. to 'A' Coy. 'C' & 'D' Coys training under own arrangements. from hospl 1OR	

WAR DIARY
or
INTELLIGENCE SUMMARY.
(Erase heading not required.)

Army Form C. 2118.

Ref. Map Sheet 45 - 1/40,000   Summary of Events and Information

Place	Date	Hour	Summary of Events and Information	Remarks and references to Appendices
MAISIERES	25/12		CHRISTMAS DAY. Voluntary church parades. Football matches & concerts under battalion arrangements. From Kopt. 2OR. from WE 10R	
" "	26/12		Forenoon devoted to filling in 'Demobilization forms' & training under battalion arrangements. From Kopt. 2OR.	
" "	27/12		Training carried out under coy arrangements. "D" Coy. 'A' by lot found guard duties at Mons station. Battalion bath ablution From Kopt. 2OR. to Kopt. 10R.	
" "	28/12		Owing to weather training carried on in billets under coy arrangements. From Kopt. 10R. to Kopt. 10R. Stand off during W 10R	

Army Form C. 2118.

WAR DIARY
or
INTELLIGENCE SUMMARY.
(Erase heading not required.)

Place	Date	Hour	Summary of Events and Information	Remarks and references to Appendices
MAISIERES	29/12	Ref. Map Sheet 45° 1:40000	Divine service held in village church at 0930. Coy inspection & C.O.s inspection of materials	
" "	30/12		Training carried out under Coy arrangement. Battalion baths allotted to 'B' Coy. to Hosp. 1.O.R.	
" "	31/12		Adjutants parade 0900-0930 C.O.'s parade & ceremonial drill at 0945 from Hosp. 2.O.R. to hospital 1.O.R.	

Summary of Casualties for December 1918.

	Increase.			Decrease.			
	O.	Ors.	Total.		O.	Ors.	Total.
Reinforcements	*1	139	140	Struck off Strength	—	5	5
From Hosp. as wounded	—	7	7	To Hospital Sick	—	42	42
" Sick	—	40	40	Died	—	1	1
Total	1	186	187	Total	—	48	48

* Capt. R.J. Dunlop.   2nd Lieut. Smith
                                                            and 1/7 Batt.

WAR DIARY or INTELLIGENCE SUMMARY

Army Form C. 2118.

1/7 H.L.I.

Vol 10

11 I.
6 sheets

Ref. Maps Sheet 45E 1/40000

Place	Date	Hour	Summary of Events and Information	Remarks and references to Appendices
MAISIÈRES	1/9		Holiday - voluntary church parade. From hospt. 1 O.R. O.W. Proceeded to U.K. for demobilization 12 O.R.	
" "	2/9		Training carried out under Coy arrangements. Proceeded to U.K. for demobilization 7 O.R.	
" "	3/9		Brigade ceremonial parade at 1000 hours on drill ground. N.W. From hospt. 1 O.R. To hospt. 2 O.R. To U.K. for demobilization 4 O.R.	
" "	4/9		Battalion ceremonial parade on drill ground. To hospt. 2 O.R. To hospt. 2 O.R. Lt Col Gartside joined unit N.W. To U.K. for demobilization 4 O.R.	
" "	5/9		Divine services Presbyterian 0920 in village hall, C of E 1145 R.C. 0845 From hospt. 7 O.R. To U.K. for Demob. 2 O.R. N.W. Receipt received from Drome 1 O.R.	

WAR DIARY or INTELLIGENCE SUMMARY

Army Form C. 2118.

Place	Date	Hour	Summary of Events and Information	Remarks and references to Appendices
MAISIERES	6/9		Ref Map Sheet 45 1/40000 Brigade Ceremonial Parade on Drill Ground at 0930. To U.K. for demobilisation 4 O.Rs.	R.B
	7/9		Training carried out under Company arrangements. To U.K. for demobilisation 4 O.Rs.	R.B
	8/9		Brigade Paper Chase. From hosp. 1 O.R.	R.B
	9/9		Brigade Group Ceremonial Parade — Presentation of M.M. & M.S.M. ribbons by Divisional Commander. From hosp. 4 O.Rs. Reinforcement 1 O.R. To U.K. for demobilisation 4 O.Rs.	R.B
	10/9		Training carried out under Company arrangements. From hosp. 2 O.Rs. To U.K. for demobilisation 8 O.Rs.	R.B

WAR DIARY
or
INTELLIGENCE SUMMARY.
(Erase heading not required.)

Army Form C. 2118.

Place	Date	Hour	Summary of Events and Information	Remarks and references to Appendices.
MASIERES	11/9		Ref map sheet 45 1:40000	
			Batalion Route March. Route: Oiao Roads on K11a - Scient Denis - Obourg. Yd hop 1 od. Serial of strength 1 od. R.B.	
	12/9		Divine Service Presbyterian at 0930 in Village hall C of E 1145. R.Cs 0845. Yd hop to Ots	R.B.
	13/9		Training carried out under Company arrangements. Yd hop 1 od.	R.B.
	14/9		Brigade Ceremonial Parade on Drill ground at 0930 3d hop 1 od.	R.B.
	15/9		Training carried out under Company arrangements. Yd hop 2 ots.	R.B.

WAR DIARY
or
INTELLIGENCE SUMMARY.

Army Form C. 2118.

(Erase heading not required.)

Place	Date	Hour	Summary of Events and Information	Remarks and references to Appendices
MAISIERES	16/9		Ref Map Sheet 45 1/40000	
			Battalion Route March. — Route traversed Cross Rds E.7.6.6. — Cross Rds E.11.a. Stren Stop. 1 OR. — Yo Stop. 1 OR.	A
"	17/9		Battalion Ceremonial Parade. Stren Stop 4 ORs. Yo Stop 4 ORs	B
"	18/9		Divisional Ceremonial Parade. Presentation of M.C.'s D.C.M's by Corps Commander. Stren Stop. 1 OR. Yo Stop 2 ORs	C
"	19/9		Divine Service — Presbyterian at 0930 in village. Full C of E 1115 — RC 0830. Yo Stop. 1 OR.	D
"	20/9		Training carried out sundry Company arrangements Stren Stop — 1 OR. Reinforcements joined from Egypt. 20 ORs.	

WAR DIARY
or
INTELLIGENCE SUMMARY.
(Erase heading not required.)

Army Form C. 2118.

Place	Date	Hour	Summary of Events and Information	Remarks and references to Appendices
MAISIERES	21/9		Ref Map Sheet 45 1/40000	
"			Training carried out under Company arrangements	D
"			40 hospital 3 O.R.S.	
"	22/9		Training carried out under Company arrangements	All
"			1 O.R. from Hop. 1 O.R. to Hop.	
"	23/9		Training carried out under Company arrangements	All
"			2 O.R. to Hop. 1 O.R. from Hop.	
"	24/9		Battalion Route March - Route - Maisieres - Tuelure - Nimy	All
"			1 O.R. from Hop. 4 O.R. to Hop.	
"	25/9		Training carried out under Company arrangements	All
"			4 O.R. to Hop.	
"	26/9		Divine Service - Presbyterians at 0900 in Village Hall	
"			C of E 1145 R.C. 0930 2 O.Rs from Hop. 1 O.R. to Hop.	
"	27/9		Training carried out under Company arrangements	All
"			1 O.R. to Hop.	

Army Form C. 2118.

WAR DIARY
or
INTELLIGENCE SUMMARY.
(Erase heading not required.)

Instructions regarding War Diaries and Intelligence Summaries are contained in F. S. Regs., Part II. and the Staff Manual respectively. Title pages will be prepared in manuscript.

Place	Date	Hour	Summary of Events and Information	Remarks and references to Appendices
MAISIERES	28/1/9		By Maj Shute +5 1-40000	
			Training carried out under Company arrangements	
	29/1/9		Training carried out under Company arrangements	
	30/1/9		Battalion Route March — Route Bras Roree via K.11 a St Denis Q304/6 Hoy	
			3 Oke from Hoy 2 OR 15 Hoy	
	31/1/9		Training carried out under Company arrangements	
			1 Reinforcement OR from U.K. 1 O.R. to Hosp. C.	

Summary of Casualties for January 1919

		O	OR	Total
Increases	Reinforcements	+1	5	6
	From hospitals wounded 1 sick 33	-	34	34
		1	39	40
Decreases	Struck off Strength Officers Attached O. Bhg Bruce Hosp. wounded 1 -49	+1	50	51
	To Hospital sick	-	30	30
		1	80	90

+ 2/Lieut L. Garnside + 2 /Lieut A.M. Bruce

Army Form C. 2118.

WAR DIARY
or
INTELLIGENCE SUMMARY.
(Erase heading not required.)

7th Bn H.L.I.

Vol 11

12 I
6 sheets

Place	Date	Hour	Summary of Events and Information	Remarks and references to Appendices
MAISIERES	1/9		Training carried out under Company arrangements	Aef
			1 Off, 1 OR to Hosp. 15 ORs to UK for Leave	
"	2/9		Divine Service — Presbyterian at 0930 in Village Hall	Nil.
			C of E 1145. R.C. 1030. 22 ORs to UK for Leave	
"	3/9		Training carried out under Company arrangements	Nil
			3 ORs to Hosp. 2 Off, 19 ORs to UK for Leave	
"	4/9		Training carried out under Company arrangements	Nil
			1 OR to Hosp.	
"	5/9		Training carried out under Company arrangements	Nil
			1 OR to Hosp. 2 ORs from Hosp.	

WAR DIARY
or
INTELLIGENCE SUMMARY.

(Erase heading not required.)

Army Form C. 2118.

Place	Date	Hour	Summary of Events and Information	Remarks and references to Appendices
MOISERES	6/2/19		Training carried out. Company arrangements. 18 O.Rs to U.K for leave	(Aug)
"	7/2/19		Training carried out. Company arrangements. 2 O.Rs to Hosp. 21 O.Rs to U.K. for leave. 20 O.Rs from Hosp.	(Aug)
"	8/2/19		Training carried out. Company arrangements. 1 O.R. to Hosp. 14 O.Rs to U.K. for leave. 1 O.R. from Hosp.	(Aug)
"	9/2/19		Divine Service — Presbyterian at 0930 in village hall. C. of E. at 1135 — R.C. 0900. 2 Off & 20 O.Rs to U.K. for leave. 1 Off & 1 O.R. from Hosp.	(Aug)
"	10/2/19		Training carried out. Company arrangements. 20 O.Rs to U.K for leave. 1 O.R. from Hosp.	(Aug)

Army Form C. 2118.

WAR DIARY
or
INTELLIGENCE SUMMARY.
(Erase heading not required.)

Instructions regarding War Diaries and Intelligence Summaries are contained in F. S. Regs., Part II. and the Staff Manual respectively. Title pages will be prepared in manuscript.

Place	Date	Hour	Summary of Events and Information	Remarks and references to Appendices
MASIÈRES	11/2/19		Training carried out under Company arrangements	OC
"	12/2/19		Training carried out under Company arrangements	OC
"	13/2/19		Training carried out under Company arrangements. 1 Off & 17 O.Rs. to U.K. for Demob.	OC
"	14/2/19		Training carried out under Company arrangements. 25 O.Rs. to U.K. for Demob. 2 O.Rs. from hosp.	OC
"	15/2/19		Training carried out under Company arrangements. 21 O.Rs. to U.K. for Demob. 2 O.Rs. from hosp.	OC

WAR DIARY or INTELLIGENCE SUMMARY.

Army Form C. 2118.

(Erase heading not required.)

Instructions regarding War Diaries and Intelligence Summaries are contained in F. S. Regs., Part II. and the Staff Manual respectively. Title pages will be prepared in manuscript.

Place	Date	Hour	Summary of Events and Information	Remarks and references to Appendices
MAISERES	16/2/19		Divine Service — Presbyterian at 0930 in Village Hall C. of E. 1145 — R.C. 0900 18 ORs to U.K. for Demob. Senior C.O./18 ORs.	
"	17/2/19		Training carried out under Company arrangements. Demob to U.K. 21 ORs	
"	18/2/19		Battalion Reorganisation	
"	19/2/19		Training carried out under Company arrangements	
"	20/2/19		Training carried out under Company arrangements. Taken off strength 10 ORs. 1 to Hosp. Demob to U.K. 23 ORs. 2 ORs from Hosp. Reinforcement 1 OR.	

Army Form. C. 2118.

WAR DIARY
or
INTELLIGENCE SUMMARY.
(Erase heading not required.)

Instructions regarding War Diaries and Intelligence Summaries are contained in F.S. Regs., Part II. and the Staff Manual respectively. Title pages will be prepared in manuscript.

Place	Date	Hour	Summary of Events and Information	Remarks and references to Appendices
MAISERES	21/3/19		Training carried out under Company arrangement. Sent to U.K. 20 O.Rs. Off strength 3 O.Rs.	AWL
"	22/3/19		Training carried out under Company arrangements. Sent to U.K. 18 O.Rs.	AWL
"	23/3/19		Divine Service — Prohibition in Village Hall at 0930. R.B. 1030 — Sent to U.K. 30 O.Rs. Off strength 1 O.R.	
"	24/3/19		Training carried out under Company arrangement. Sent to U.K. 6 O.Rs.	AWL
"	25/3/19		Training carried out under Company arrangement. Struck off strength 15 O.Rs.	AWL

WAR DIARY
or
INTELLIGENCE SUMMARY.

(Erase heading not required.)

Army Form C. 2118.

Place	Date	Hour	Summary of Events and Information	Remarks and references to Appendices
MAISIÈRES	26/2/19		Training carried out under Company arrangements. Group Staff. I.O.R.	AK2
	27/2/19		Training carried out under Company arrangements. Send to W.K. GOE.	AK2
	28/2/19		Training carried out under Company arrangements. Send to W.K. 2 O.R.	AK2

Summary of Casualties for February 1919

	O.	O.R.	Total	Decreases	O.	O.R.	Total
				Recruit off strength Leave absents O–98 Y 388 Sicks 16 u.K.— Y 388	Y	403	410
Reinforcements	—	1	1		—	11	11
Sick Hos/Hos/sick 13	—	13	13		Y	414	421
	—	14	14				

(A9175) Wt W2358/P366 60,000 12/17 D. D. & L. Sch. 52a. Forms/Can8/15.

1/4th A.K.I.

WAR DIARY
or
INTELLIGENCE SUMMARY.

Army Form C. 2118.

13 I
7 sheets

Place	Date	Hour	Summary of Events and Information	Remarks and references to Appendices
MAISERES	1/3/19		Training carried out under company arrangements	
"	2/3/19		Leaving from Hospital 1 OR	
"	3/19		Divine Service - Probyterian at 0930 in Village Hall	
"	3/19		Training carried out under company arrangements	
"	4/3/19		To Hospital 2 ORs	
"	4/3/19		Training carried out under company arrangements	
"	5/3/19		Training carried out under company arrangements	
"			To Hospital 1 OR	

WAR DIARY
or
INTELLIGENCE SUMMARY.
(Erase heading not required.)

Army Form C. 2118.

Place	Date	Hour	Summary of Events and Information	Remarks and references to Appendices
MAISIERES	6/3/19		Training carried out under Company arrangements	MB
"	7/3/19		Training carried out under Company arrangements. Proceeded to U.K. for Demobilisation 1 Officer	MB
"	8/3/19		Training carried out under Company arrangements. 2 O.Rs. Proceeded to U.K. for Demobilisation. 30/R Transferred to B.A.R. 2 O.Rs. Transferred from 1/9 Hospital 1 O.R.	MB
"	9/3/19	0930	Divine Service — Presbyterian in Village Hall ac	
"	10/3/19		From Hospital 3 O.Rs. Reinforcements from Bde 1 O.R. Training carried out under Company arrangements	MB

Army Form C. 2118.

WAR DIARY
or
INTELLIGENCE SUMMARY.
(Erase heading not required.)

Place	Date	Hour	Summary of Events and Information	Remarks and references to Appendices
Maroeuil	11/3/19		Training carried out under Company arrangements	MO
"	12/3/19		Training carried out under Company arrangements	MO
"	13/3/19		Training carried out under Company arrangements	MO
"	14/3/19		Training carried out under Company arrangements for educational duty officers 2/L R.R. first to Hospital 10R	R
"	15/3/19		Inspection of Army of Occupation draft by L own aubing officer Don Hospital 10R	R

Army Form C. 2118.

WAR DIARY
or
INTELLIGENCE SUMMARY.
(Erase heading not required.)

Instructions regarding War Diaries and Intelligence Summaries are contained in F. S. Regs., Part II. and the Staff Manual respectively. Title pages will be prepared in manuscript.

Place	Date	Hour	Summary of Events and Information	Remarks and references to Appendices
Maisoncelle	16/3/19		Divine Service – Presbyterian in Village Hall at 10.00. Proceeded to UK for Demobilisation 2/Offrs 2/Lt R. Bunn 7 O.Rs	nil
"	17/3/19		Departure of Army of Occupation Draft 14.00. Relieved by E. & L. Y.R. Proceeded to 19 H.L.I. 6 Offrs & 15 O.R.s — both Staffs 2/Lt Variley 2/Lt Hanby 2/Lt Park, Esty in Zm. Engley, 2/Lt Mottram, 2/Lt & G/Lt. Proceeded to UK for Demobilisation 2/Offrs 2/Lt Crawford 1 & 5.O.Rs 2/Lt O/G/Lt Littlely J/C O'Connell	Y.R.
"	18/3/19		Cadre 1 from Hospital 1 O.R.	Y.R.
"	19/3/19		Cadre 1 from Embarkation Duty 2/Lt C. Boast	Y.R.
"	20/3/19		Cadre 1 from Embarkation Duty 2/Lt G. Antsloch 1 from Base 1 O.R.	

(A9173) Wt W235/P363 500,000 12/17 D. D. & L. Sch. 52a. Forms/C2118/15.

Army Form C. 2118.

WAR DIARY
or
INTELLIGENCE SUMMARY.
(Erase heading not required.)

Instructions regarding War Diaries and Intelligence Summaries are contained in F. S. Regs., Part II. and the Staff Manual respectively. Title pages will be prepared in manuscript.

Place	Date	Hour	Summary of Events and Information	Remarks and references to Appendices
Morcourt	21/3/19		Cadre moved to billets in Sorgnies	JR
			3 O.Rs struck off strength	
Sorgnies	22/3/19		Cadre	JR
			Proceeded to U.K. for Demobilisation 1 O.R.	
Sorgnies	23/3/19		Cadre	JR
Sorgnies	24/3/19		Cadre	JR
Sorgnies	25/3/19		Cadre 1 O.R. from Hospital	JR

WAR DIARY
or
INTELLIGENCE SUMMARY.
(Erase heading not required.)

Army Form C. 2118.

Place	Date	Hour	Summary of Events and Information	Remarks and references to Appendices
Soignies	26/3/19		Cadre	sgd
Soignies	27/3/19		Cadre 4 Officers & 2 O.Rs demobilized 1 Officer struck off strength 1 Officer to Hospital	sgd
Soignies	28/3/19		Cadre 6 Officers & 2 O.Rs demobilized 1 O.R. to Hospital	
Soignies	29/3/19		Cadre. 3 O.Rs struck off strength	
Soignies	30/3/19		Cadre 1 Officer & 9 O.R to Army of Occupation	
Soignies	31/3/19		Cadre 1. O.R reinforcement	

WAR DIARY
or
INTELLIGENCE SUMMARY.
(Erase heading not required.)

Army Form C. 2118.

Summary of Casualties for March 1919.

Increases.

	O.	ORs	Total
Reinforcements	3	3	
From Hospital	7	7	
	10	10	

Decreases.

	O.	ORs	Total
Struck off Strength	2	8	10
To Hospital	1	6	7
Demobilised	15	20	35
To Army of Occupation	9	168	177
	27	202	229

Gauton

LIEUT.-COLONEL
COMMDG 7TH H.L.I.

Gailes
15-5-19.

The Secretary
War Office
London

Herewith A.F.C. 2118 for the month of April, 19. sent direct to you, as Brigade Headquarters have not yet arrived here.

1/7TH BATTALION,
HIGHLAND
LIGHT INFANTRY.
No. W 10
Date 15-5-19.

G. A. Cuddeford
Lt. & Adjt.
1/7 H.L.I.

1/7th H.L.I.
April 1919.

WAR DIARY
or
INTELLIGENCE SUMMARY.
(Erase heading not required.)

Army Form C. 2118.

Place	Date	Hour	Summary of Events and Information	Remarks and references to Appendices
Sergines	1/4/19		1 O.R. to Hospital	Gal
"	2/4/19		6 O.Rs to U.K. for demobilisation	Gal
"	"		1 O.R. from Hospital	Gal
"	9/4/19		2 O.Rs to Hospital	Gal
"	10/4/19		5 O.Rs struck off strength (Posted to 15th H.L.I.)	Gal
"	"		8 O.Rs " " " (" " 9th A.C.9)	Gal
"	12/4/19		1 O.R. from Hospital	Gal
"	14/4/19		1 O.R. to U.K. for demobilisation	Gal
"	18/4/19		2/Lt. C. Bisset transferred to 9th Scottish Rifles	Gal

Army Form C. 2118.

WAR DIARY
or
INTELLIGENCE SUMMARY.
(Erase heading not required.)

Place	Date	Hour	Summary of Events and Information	Remarks and references to Appendices
Soignies	19/4/19		1 O.R to Hospital	C.M.C
"	23/4/19		1 O.R to Hospital	C.M.C
"	28/4/19		2 O.Rs to U.K. for demobilization	C.M.C
Dunkirk	30/4/19		2 O.Rs Struck off strength (Posted to 9th H.L.I)	C.M.C
			Summary of Casualties for April 1919	
			Decreases — O / O.Rs / Total Increases — O / O.Rs / Total	
			Struck off Strength — 1 / 15 / 16 From Hospital — — / 2 / 2	
			To Hospital — — / 5 / 5	
			Demobilized — — / 9 / 9	
			Total — 1 / 29 / 30 Total — — / 2 / 2	
Gailes	1/5/19		Cadre demobilized	C.M.C

Lieut. Gertrude Vent. Colonel
Comdg. 9th Batt. H.L.I.

www.ingramcontent.com/pod-product-compliance
Lightning Source LLC
Chambersburg PA
CBHW081411160426
43193CB00013B/2153